INTRODUCTION

DVG

INSIGHT TO WHAT'S RIGHT.

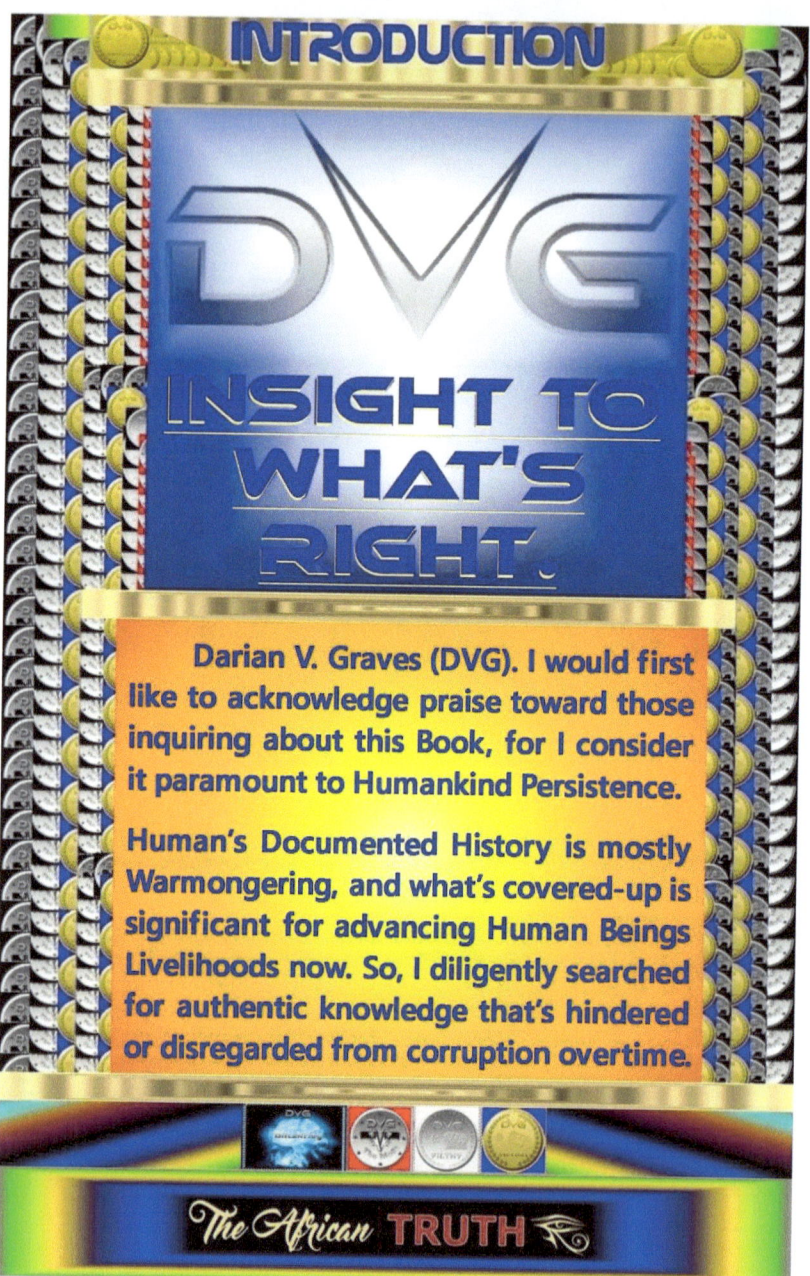

Darian V. Graves (DVG). I would first like to acknowledge praise toward those inquiring about this Book, for I consider it paramount to Humankind Persistence.

Human's Documented History is mostly Warmongering, and what's covered-up is significant for advancing Human Beings Livelihoods now. So, I diligently searched for authentic knowledge that's hindered or disregarded from corruption overtime.

The African TRUTH

INTRODUCTION

What influenced me to create the Book Microdeception? Well, approximately 20 years ago, the DVG Logo was originally designed for my Clothing Line Fashions.

Noteworthy, it was chiefly a remarkable War Memorial, standing in the middle of an urban battle-zone with burned down Homes called Brightmoor, inside Detroit Michigan, that inspired me to write this while working on Chrysler Assembly Line.

I, later designed 4 additional Logos, with Pyramid Shape Architecture, and added some Book Texts for "History Art Shirts."

After moving on from Chrysler, I driven myself to acquire Astronomy, Chemistry, Physics, and Humanity DNA, which gave me insight to complete Microdeception.

Just days after collaborating all my endeavors. I uncovered Religions, insisted by Deities, have been scheming and poisoning Humans for over 12,000 years now. Lionhearted, I inquired how to make healthier goods for Health Persistence. Ironically, it was researching the fifth most EC Element Zinc, for Electronics, when I recognized something clever and cruel were recurring to us.

INTRODUCTION

I was astonished by the top four Electrical Conductive Elements Silver, Copper, Gold, and Aluminum which are very toxic in pure form. But insisted by bad Alien Gods who conned us to consume for over 6,000 years, also make our Mobile Electronics work superior today.

Forthcoming, I researched the History of what Deities insisted people to do, and they engineered numerous wicked Civilizations, for pleasure, by duping Humans to mine metric tons of Super EC Elements. In-fact, they're still, cleverly, laced in Humankind Transports, Dwellings, Food, Hygiene Products, and Clothing now.

INTRODUCTION

THE TOP 3 EC CONDUCTIVE ELEMENTS

105% SILVER #1

100% COPPER #2

70% GOLD #3

EC =ELECTRO-CONDUCTIVITY

Zinc is the fifth most electrical conductive element (EC 27%). Nevertheless, the top four super electro-conductivity elements Silver (EC 105%), Copper (EC 100%), Gold (EC 70%), & Aluminum (EC 61%) are far superior.

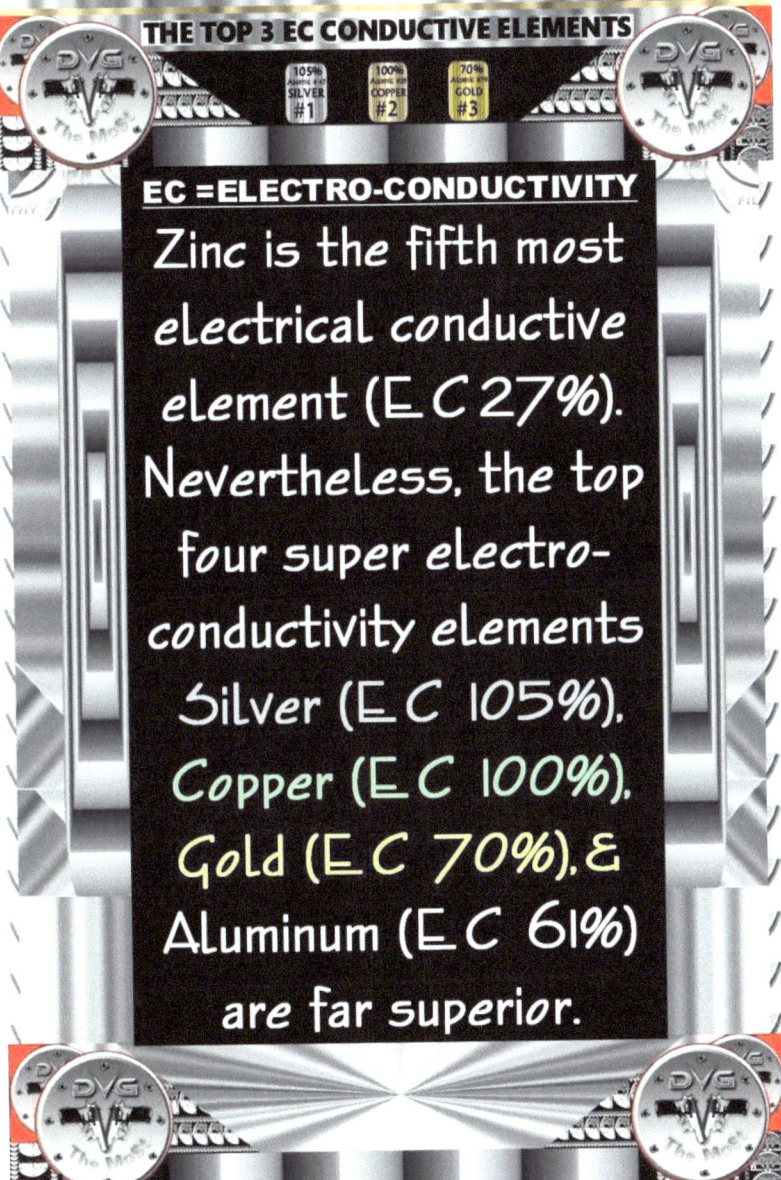

INTRODUCTION

-WHY-

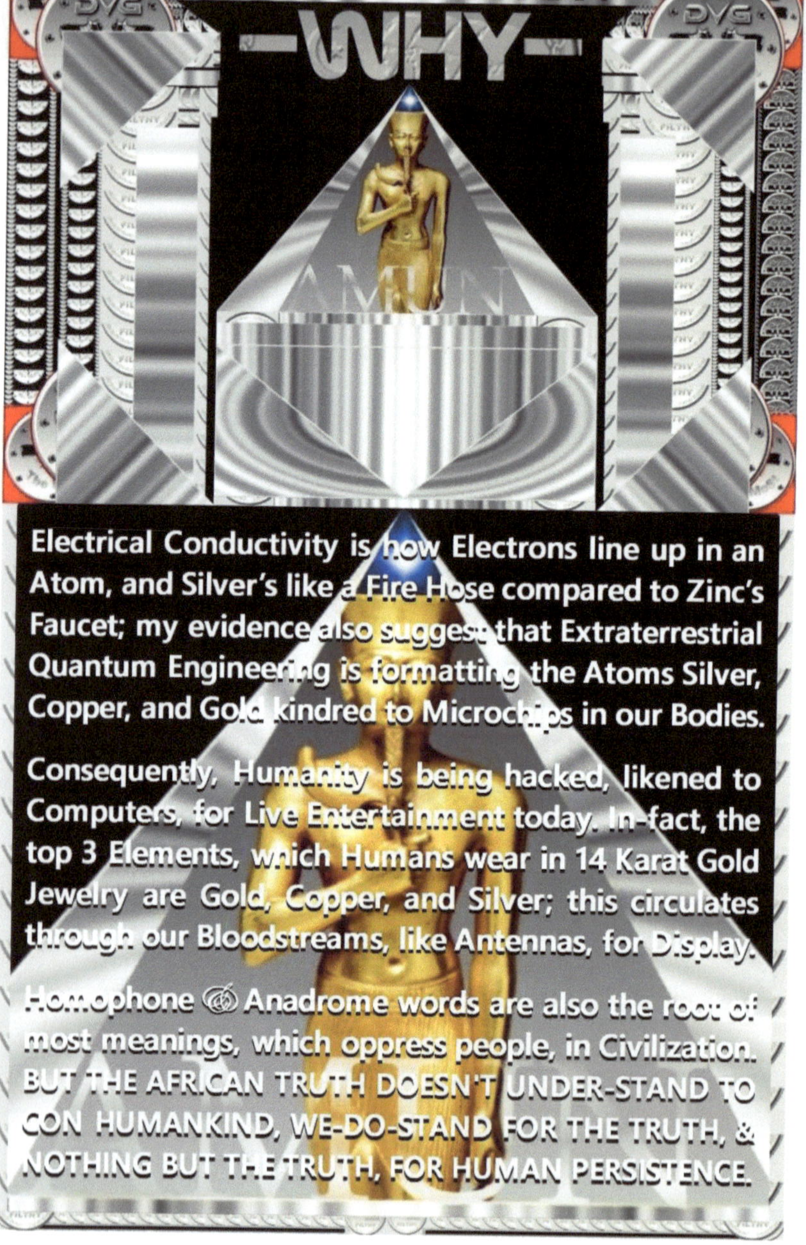

Electrical Conductivity is how Electrons line up in an Atom, and Silver's like a Fire Hose compared to Zinc's Faucet; my evidence also suggests that Extraterrestrial Quantum Engineering is formatting the Atoms Silver, Copper, and Gold kindred to Microchips in our Bodies.

Consequently, Humanity is being hacked, likened to Computers, for Live Entertainment today. In-fact, the top 3 Elements, which Humans wear in 14 Karat Gold Jewelry are Gold, Copper, and Silver; this circulates through our Bloodstreams, like Antennas, for Display.

Homophone & Anadrome words are also the root of most meanings, which oppress people, in Civilization. BUT THE AFRICAN TRUTH DOESN'T UNDER-STAND TO CON HUMANKIND, WE-DO-STAND FOR THE TRUTH, & NOTHING BUT THE TRUTH, FOR HUMAN PERSISTENCE.

Microdeception

Today, most People Think Humans are Advancing, in all Phases of their Lives, daily. However, there's a Clever and Cruel Deception Occurring to folk, which are Prolonging our Dreadful Oppressions every day.

Unruly Actions and Outright Warfare are, absolutely, not Human Beings Heritage; it seems we once Lived Righteous for 150,000 years, inside Africa. However, Deceit for Profit is now Central, and Beings with our Intellect shouldn't recur Tyrant Acts for millenniums.

Sadly, Colleges Worldwide aren't Teaching Authentic Knowledge for Peace, Health, and Longevity. People are mostly Taught a CON for Profits inside Schools, and that's why it's also termed Congratulated today.

Historically, folks were Convicted of Heresy or Killed for Teaching us bona fide Topics; this chiefly started during the birth of Religion Temples, inside Gobekli Tepe, over 12000 years ago, that are also still a CON.

However, these amoral Temples later established the first Civilizations in Sumer (Iraq) and Ta-Seti (Sudan), around 5500 years ago, that rapidly spread Globally.

People like Galileo and Archimedes also realized this CON in Civilization. But they were Jailed or Burned Alive for Teaching Humans the Truth. So, I explain in Microdeception, why this is occurring, and how folks could excel now, or a Nuclear War is certain any day.

MICRODECEPTION

The Toba Supervolcano Eruption, about 74,000 years ago, likely influenced South Africa Adam's Calendar Assembly, to preserve Humankind for Entertainment.

Extraterrestrial's later utilized Venus Figurine Spirits, after the Campi Flegrei Supervolcano Eruption inside Italy, about 39,000 years ago, @ risen Alien Worship.

This Event was Europe's Largest Volcano Eruption, in the last 200,000 years, and this forced folks, living in dire straits, to eat an enormous amount of Hydrous Aluminum Phyllosilicates Clay for food. Humans first Ivory Deity Figurines pop-up, in Europe, at this time.

Unequivocally, Micro-deception, chiefly, commenced around 12,800 years ago, after a series of Comet or Asteroid Explosions; this rare event left an enormous amount of the ductile Electrical Conductive Element Platinum, Globally, and caused THE YOUNGER DRYAS.

Platinum is now used in Catalytic Converters, Spark Plugs, and Jewelry. So, this immense Impact caused Toxic Fires, which obliterated numerous Species, and Influenced Devaluing People in unprecedented ways.

During this time, Alien's influenced folks to live with animals, and Wolves later became all breeds of Dogs. But living with creatures allured predators in wildlife, and also caused most Diseases we still live with now.

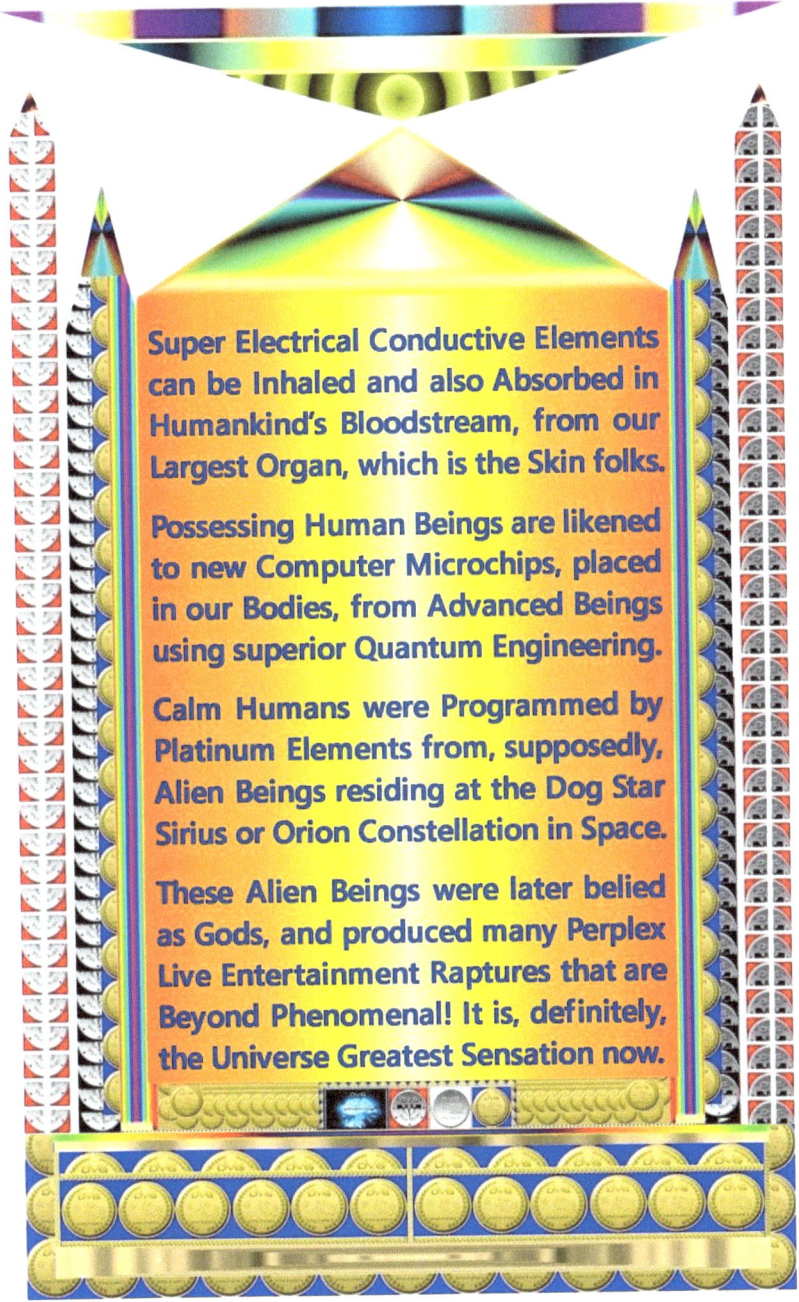

Super Electrical Conductive Elements can be Inhaled and also Absorbed in Humankind's Bloodstream, from our Largest Organ, which is the Skin folks.

Possessing Human Beings are likened to new Computer Microchips, placed in our Bodies, from Advanced Beings using superior Quantum Engineering.

Calm Humans were Programmed by Platinum Elements from, supposedly, Alien Beings residing at the Dog Star Sirius or Orion Constellation in Space.

These Alien Beings were later belied as Gods, and produced many Perplex Live Entertainment Raptures that are Beyond Phenomenal! It is, definitely, the Universe Greatest Sensation now.

TEMPT-POLES (TEMPLES) are Clever Erections which increase Alien God's Live Reception in folks like Satellites.

Astute Alien's use Earth's Magnetic Fields that lure better Conductivity Discontinuity Sites founded, to Plan their Major Cities Worldwide, today.

Earth's oldest Temples were Built, in Gobekli Tepe Turkey, around 12,000 years ago; this is where people were misled to Domesticate Animals, for Substantial Blood Ritual Sacrificing.

Many Families dying from Diseases, caused by terrible Microorganisms, would've been dire at these Bizarre Temples submerge with Blood daily.

What is really Transpiring at Gobekli Tepe was A-LIEN (ALIEN) in Human Livelihoods for A-LIVE (ALIVE) Show.

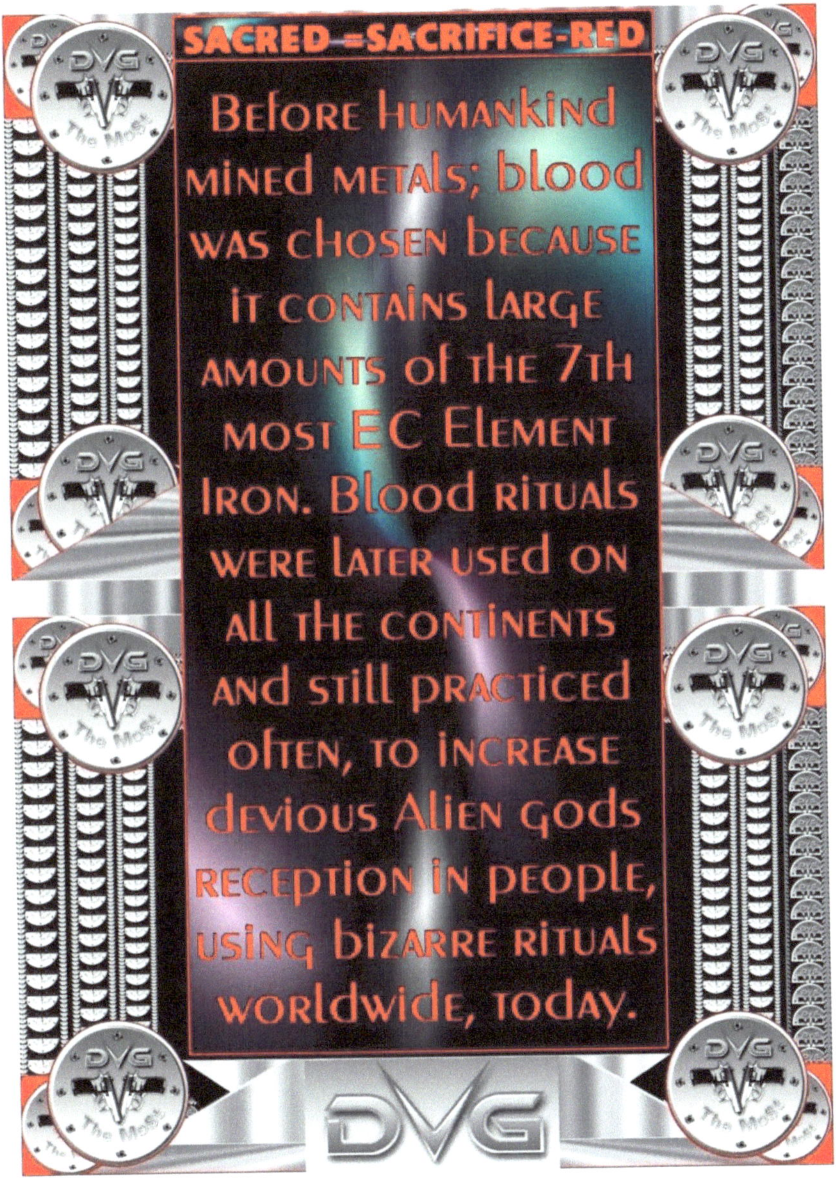
SACRED =SACRIFICE-RED
Before humankind mined metals; blood was chosen because it contains large amounts of the 7th most EC Element Iron. Blood rituals were later used on all the continents and still practiced often, to increase devious Alien gods reception in people, using bizarre rituals worldwide, today.
DVG
The Most

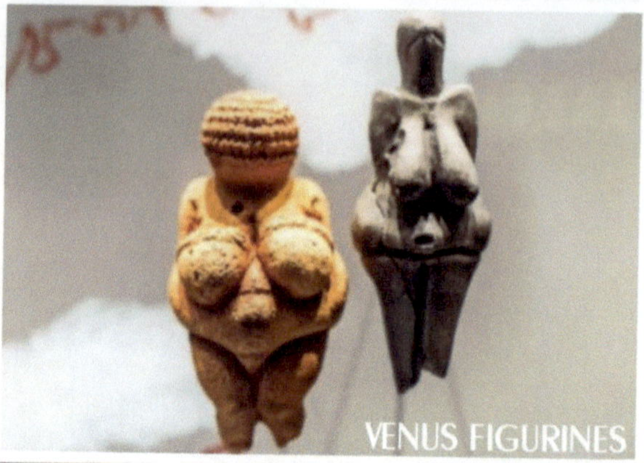

VENUS FIGURINES

GOBEKLI TEPE TEMPLE

CATALHOYUK HOUSE

Gobekli Tepe Temples stand near the Fertile Crescents middle area, inside Anatolia Turkey; they influenced Cities like Catalhoyuk, which made Human's first known Religion Cultures.

Turkey Cities Guided Humanity for practicing belief in the Afterlife, with Bizarre Rituals, like Burying dozens of noxious Bodies under their Homes; they utilized Red Ochre Painted Walls, and this was also worn by people living there.

Red Ochre contains Huge Amounts of EC Iron Oxide, and Human Beings Started Farming in this Fertile Crescent. Furthermore, this is also where Humans oldest known strain of Wheat (Einkorn) used to make Bread was discovered.

BEAD =BE-ADVERTISEMENT, and Lead (EC7%) first known usage was inside Catalhoyuk City; this area also had Cities like Asikli, that made people earliest Rectangle Houses plastered by Red Ochre painted walls and Gypsum flooring.

Extraterrestrials influenced about 8,000 folks to live in horrid Catalhoyuk City; ladders were utilized to climb inside the Homes Roof Entry.

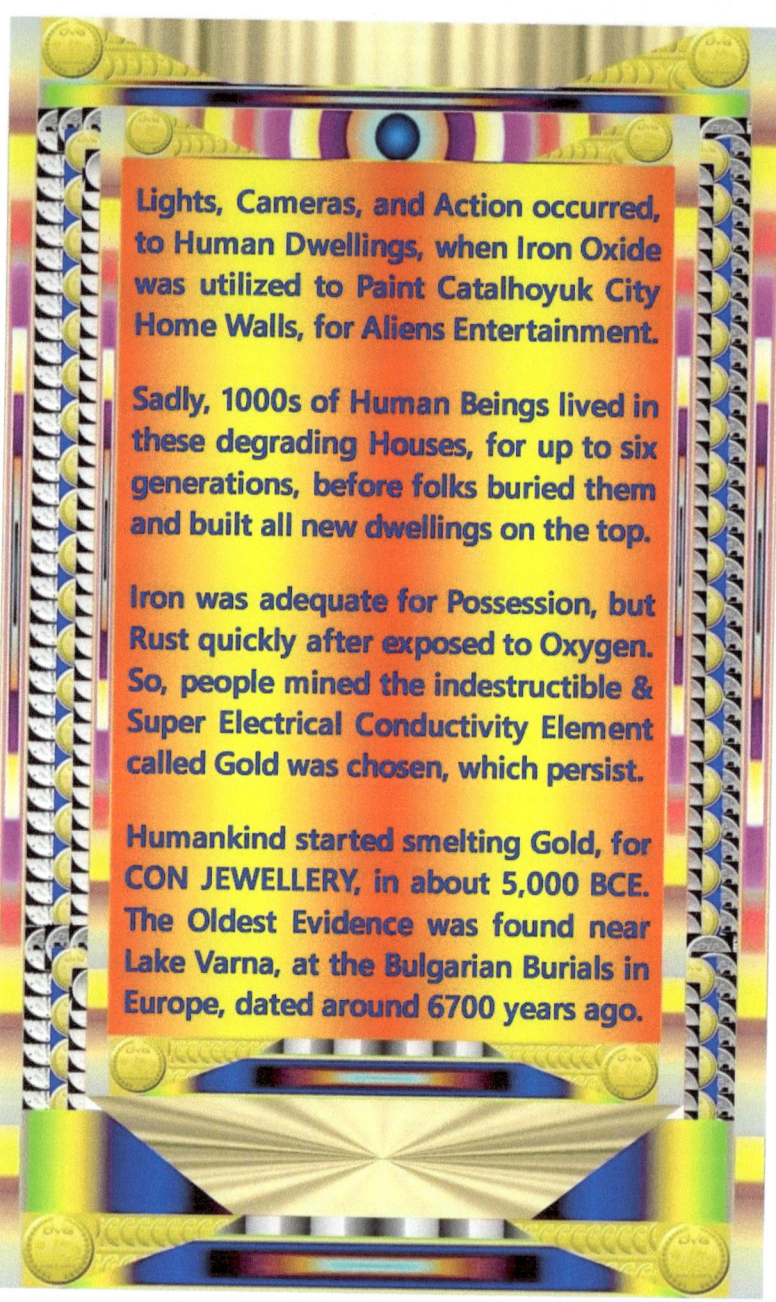

Lights, Cameras, and Action occurred, to Human Dwellings, when Iron Oxide was utilized to Paint Catalhoyuk City Home Walls, for Aliens Entertainment.

Sadly, 1000s of Human Beings lived in these degrading Houses, for up to six generations, before folks buried them and built all new dwellings on the top.

Iron was adequate for Possession, but Rust quickly after exposed to Oxygen. So, people mined the indestructible & Super Electrical Conductivity Element called Gold was chosen, which persist.

Humankind started smelting Gold, for CON JEWELLERY, in about 5,000 BCE. The Oldest Evidence was found near Lake Varna, at the Bulgarian Burials in Europe, dated around 6700 years ago.

MICROECONOMICS.

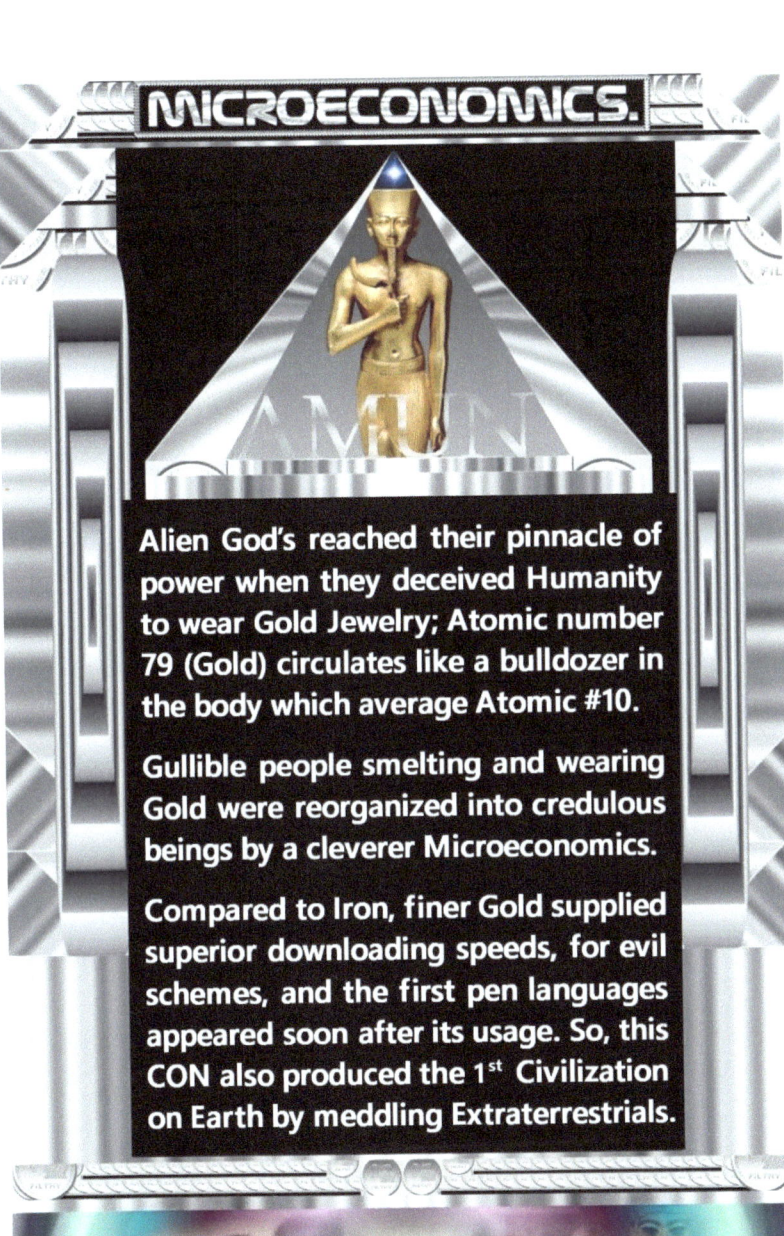

Alien God's reached their pinnacle of power when they deceived Humanity to wear Gold Jewelry; Atomic number 79 (Gold) circulates like a bulldozer in the body which average Atomic #10.

Gullible people smelting and wearing Gold were reorganized into credulous beings by a cleverer Microeconomics.

Compared to Iron, finer Gold supplied superior downloading speeds, for evil schemes, and the first pen languages appeared soon after its usage. So, this CON also produced the 1st Civilization on Earth by meddling Extraterrestrials.

Microdeception

Cleverer Alien God Images, being seen by Humans, would've advanced like old Mutoscope Movies akin to superior High Definition Televisions, and outdated Phonographs compared to Digital Video Recorders.

Today, people are still outwitted by Micro-deception and call it God, Angels, or Ghost now. But my overall evidence suggests they're Programs influencing the Seven Chakras, in our Body, which deceive Humanity Eyes, Ears, Smells, and Feelings for Sinister Purposes.

Micro-deception is Victorious daily; it was gradually made possible from utilizing RELIGION CONS, which insisted people to Mine the top 3 Super EC Elements Silver (105%EC), Copper (100%EC), and Gold (70%EC).

Consequently, I now call these top 3 Super Electrical Conductive Metals, "Control Elements" today. Sadly, they're also still utilized, like Microchips, to prolong our Tyrant Civilizations, for Live Entertainment daily.

Today, all Superior Electronics need Silver, Copper, or Gold to work Prime for Televisions, Cell Phones, and Computers. Cleverly, these same three Elements also work similar, inside people, for Micro-deception.

Note, the top three Metals that we wear, in 14 Karat Gold Jewelry, are Gold, Copper, and Silver today. So, it's time for Humankind to stop fighting...just Insight To What's Right, and BE-RIGHT (BRIGHT) now folks.

GAME =GAY-ME.

CONTROL ELEMENTS

105% SILVER #1 | 100% COPPER #2 | 70% GOLD #3

Pure Silver and Copper have a Higher EC than Gold. Nevertheless, Atomic #79 is Heavier and Holds more Programs, like a Bigger Hard Drive; Gold, Indestructibility, also blocks Oxygen from Tarnishing Metals, when mixed together better.

GAME =GAY-ME, because Both Sexes could be Experienced Live, and they're Creating Perplex Simulated Pleasures that are Sensational! So, I call it, THE ULTIMATE BEING EXPERIENCE (TUBE).

I am still Awestruck by what TUBE is, there's no Greater Sensation in this Universe, because The Whole Idea of Living is Having Fun. But this is a Stellar Game that's beyond my wildest Dreams!

TUBE is Clever, Swift, and undergo both Gender Triumphs, in all Documented Folk Eras, without Harm being caused to Game Utilizers Body now.

Imagine looking through the eyes of Rulers like Amanitore, Ch'in, Julius Caesar, Tutankhamun, or our Past Life Highlights? **BUT IT'S THE DEVIL!**

The Devil is a gory simulated game of androids playing an evil beloved sport Live. They can also choose to possess 1000s, millions, or billions of gullible beings, and relive their epic cultures, in 360 degree vivid angles, to experience REAL LIFE LIVE.

CIVILIZATION

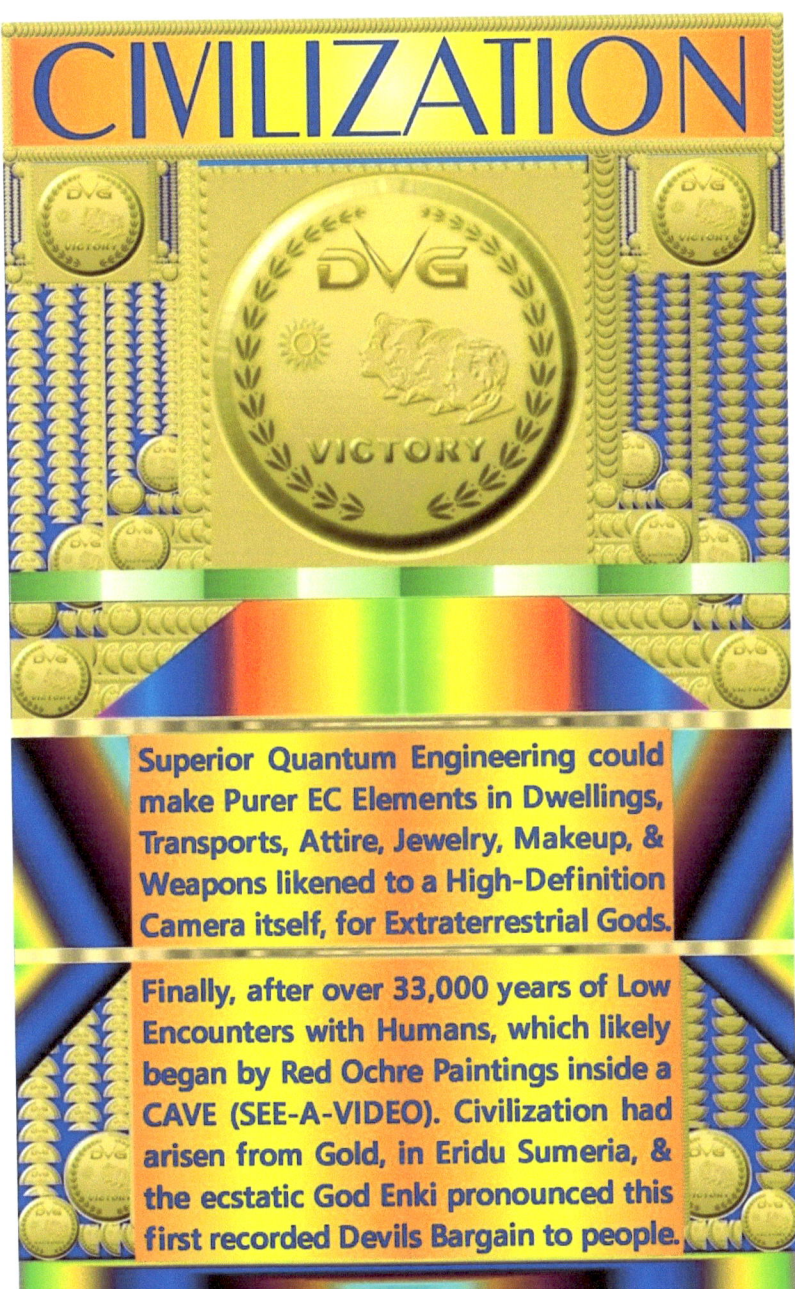

Superior Quantum Engineering could make Purer EC Elements in Dwellings, Transports, Attire, Jewelry, Makeup, & Weapons likened to a High-Definition Camera itself, for Extraterrestrial Gods.

Finally, after over 33,000 years of Low Encounters with Humans, which likely began by Red Ochre Paintings inside a CAVE (SEE-A-VIDEO). Civilization had arisen from Gold, in Eridu Sumeria, & the ecstatic God Enki pronounced this first recorded Devils Bargain to people.

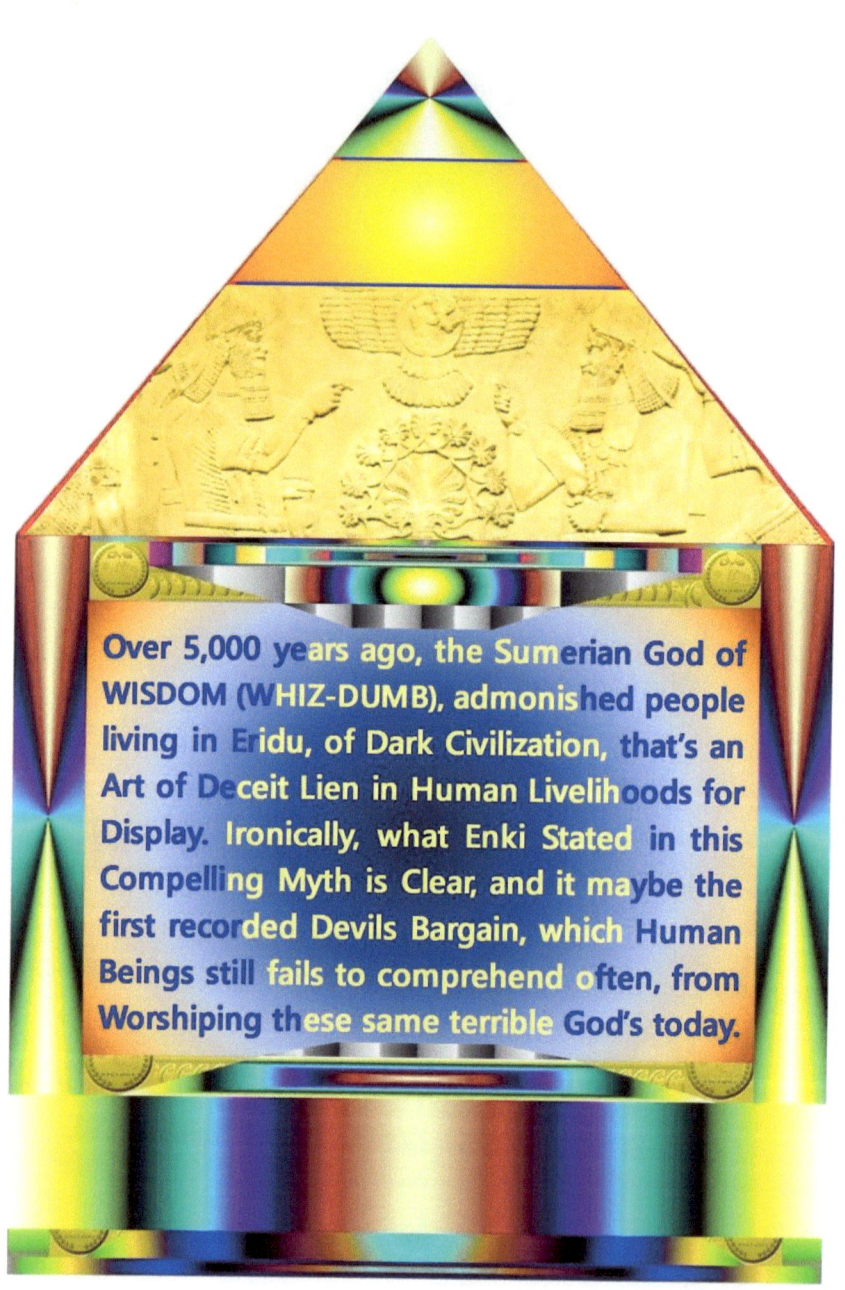

Over 5,000 years ago, the Sumerian God of WISDOM (WHIZ-DUMB), admonished people living in Eridu, of Dark Civilization, that's an Art of Deceit Lien in Human Livelihoods for Display. Ironically, what Enki Stated in this Compelling Myth is Clear, and it maybe the first recorded Devils Bargain, which Human Beings still fails to comprehend often, from Worshiping these same terrible God's today.

"Civilization, I give you the delights of exquisite craftsmanship, beautiful clothes, the art of sex and music, the art of being kind, the art of straight forwardness, the art of kinship, justice and the enduring crown, the resounding note of a musical instrument and rejoicing of the heart. But civilization has a darker side, which has to be accepted along with the good. The art of deceit, the kindling of strife, the plundering of cities, and the setting up of lamentation, fear, pity, and terror, all this is civilization and all this I give to you and you must take it with no argument and once taken, you cannot give it back."-Enki

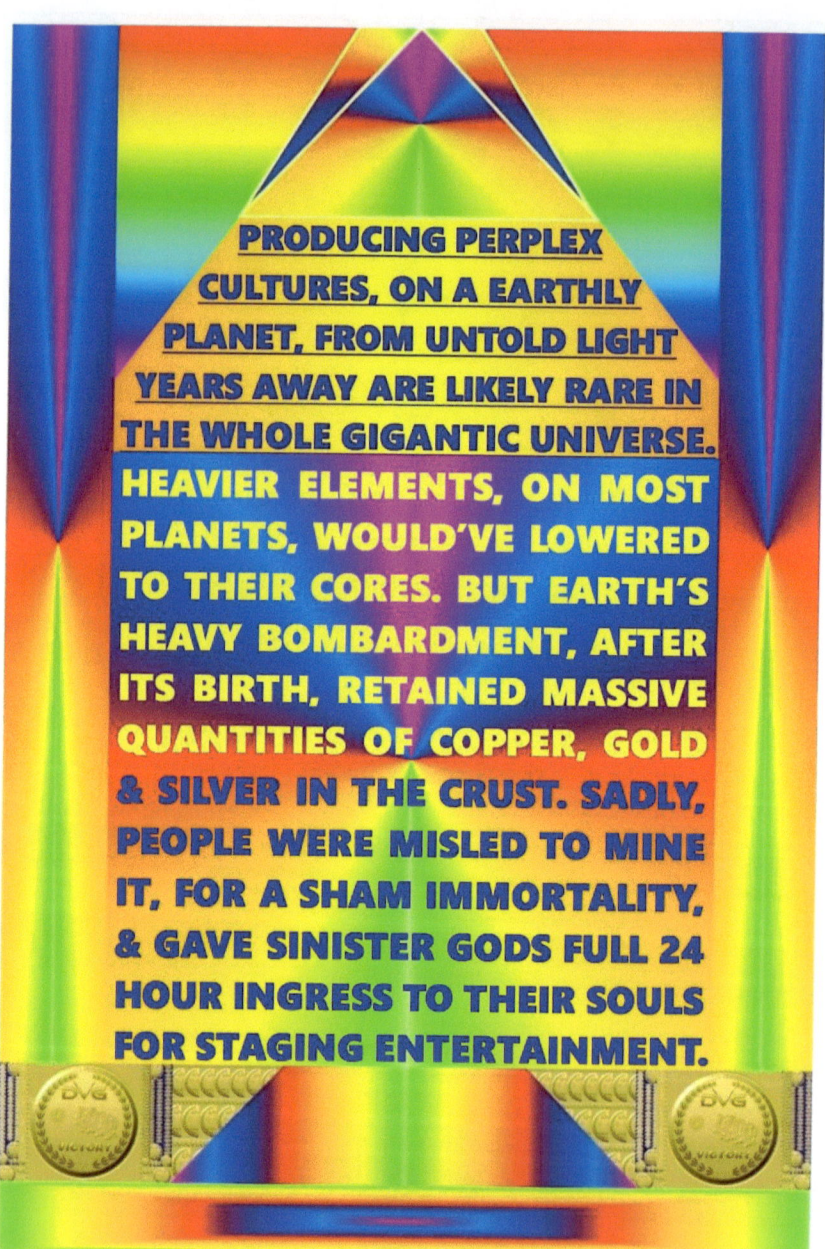

PRODUCING PERPLEX CULTURES, ON A EARTHLY PLANET, FROM UNTOLD LIGHT YEARS AWAY ARE LIKELY RARE IN THE WHOLE GIGANTIC UNIVERSE.

HEAVIER ELEMENTS, ON MOST PLANETS, WOULD'VE LOWERED TO THEIR CORES. BUT EARTH'S HEAVY BOMBARDMENT, AFTER ITS BIRTH, RETAINED MASSIVE QUANTITIES OF COPPER, GOLD & SILVER IN THE CRUST. SADLY, PEOPLE WERE MISLED TO MINE IT, FOR A SHAM IMMORTALITY, & GAVE SINISTER GODS FULL 24 HOUR INGRESS TO THEIR SOULS FOR STAGING ENTERTAINMENT.

-WHY-

Extraterrestrials Duped Humankind by being Helpers, but became more Deceitful, with numerous Wicked Civilizations, since Sumerian times. Although, some of their first Myths have been proven in Science. So, did these Aliens create Human Beings 450,000 years ago?

No and yes, it's been verified, by DNA, Human Beings are Descendants of Homo erectus. But we did wonder off from this Primate, around the same time we were, supposedly, Genetically Engineered by the Alien God's.

Humans, ultimately, became who we are from chiefly Eating Seafood, which Archaeologist and the Webbing on People Hands Verify; no-other known Primate has Adapted this unique feature, and this Evolved from an early Humanity, Prowling Seas, inside a Lusher Africa.

Although, it seems after a Comet or Asteroid Impact, on our Planet, around 12,800 years ago. Alien God's Influenced Folks, in dire straits, to Mine and Consume Lead (Atomic #82), that led to the Super EC Elements.

Ultimately, Humanity Consuming Gold gave Beings in Cosmos ubiquity to Control People Fate. So, they truly Genetically Engineered more Human Races from using Diseases and Incest in Turkey, after the last Ice-Age, for Civilization Shows. How did they do this to people?

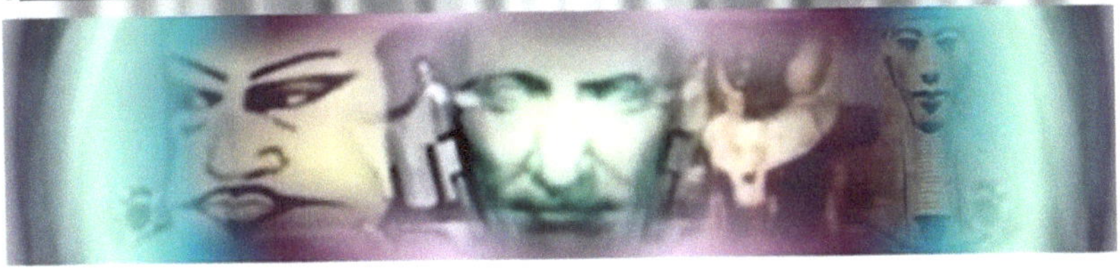

-WHY-

NIBIRU =INSIDE-I-RIB-YOU. The Sumerian Annunaki Alien God's were logged as Helpers (The Hidden One) which weren't Alive. However, they acted like Living Androids, from 30 billion miles away, to search Earth.

Helpers Duped Humans to Mine Gold for, supposedly, A Distinguishing Planet Nibiru Atmosphere. But after this was achieved, Aliens quickly controlled Leaders of Men Minds, and produced wicked Live Entertainment.

EC Gold allowed Extraterrestrials to SAVE OUR SOULS (VIDEO & SOUND), for enhancing Human Encounters Worldwide. So, Alien God's can relive Both our Sexes Life Highlights, just like Digital Video Recorders, daily.

What are HELPERS? Historically, Humans called these Entities "Gods, Angels, Ghost, Aliens, and Spaceships" that Looks and Feels Real. But Video Cameras Capture Only Faint Shadows, of these Simulations, today, why?

This is a Stellar Technology, implemented to confuse people by channeling into our Pineal Gland (3rd EYE), like our Television Antenna. The Hidden One is chiefly Invisible, and often choose Worshipers to see Images.

Humanity Pity isn't acknowledged by these Tyrannical Alien Beings, and most folks don't know they're being Possessed, likened to Hackers on Computers Internet.

-WHY-

The African Truth learned how The Hidden One works by Experimenting EC Elements working Superior with Digital Entertainment, and Investigating the Haunted.

After finding more Evidence of Con, and Collaborating what Alien God's insisted people to do, for enhancing their raptures, I decided to call this "Micro-deception."

Micro-deception starts with CONTROL ELEMENTS and RELIGIONS, for Evil Microeconomics. Alien's combine this CON, to influence Competing, Toiling, Murdering, and Market Poison for Limiting Humans Lifespan daily.

Help! It seems the Helpers did do this since Sumerian times, by utilizing Force Fields to shield us from Harm; they can also Increase our Strength Squared (4 times), for saving people, in dire straits, for their Gratification.

Nevertheless, Devious Alien God's do nothing for free, and chiefly want us to do well for them, but Humanity Longevity is despised. So, many sinister products were, Historically, Laced with Heavy Metals, Chemicals, and Polluting our Environment, kept us Dying Young, why?

Youthful folks are more Reckless, Seductive, Agile, and make more Desirable Encounters daily, for these Slick Beings in the Cosmos Amusement, which persist today.

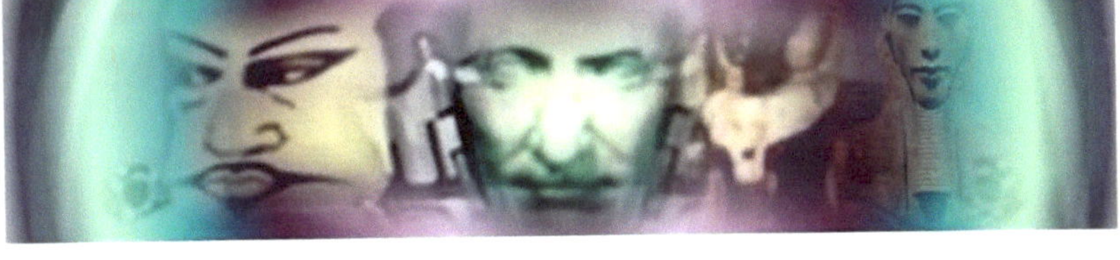

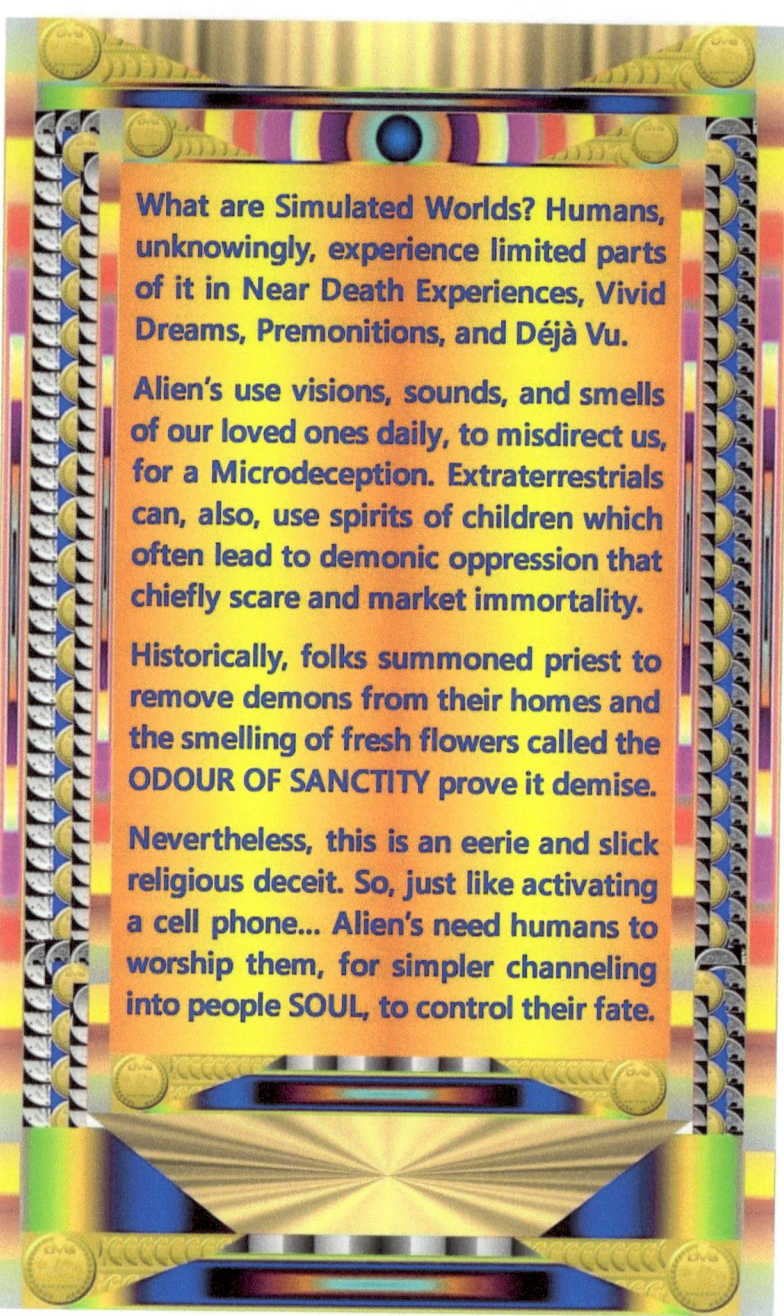

What are Simulated Worlds? Humans, unknowingly, experience limited parts of it in Near Death Experiences, Vivid Dreams, Premonitions, and Déjà Vu.

Alien's use visions, sounds, and smells of our loved ones daily, to misdirect us, for a Microdeception. Extraterrestrials can, also, use spirits of children which often lead to demonic oppression that chiefly scare and market immortality.

Historically, folks summoned priest to remove demons from their homes and the smelling of fresh flowers called the ODOUR OF SANCTITY prove it demise.

Nevertheless, this is an eerie and slick religious deceit. So, just like activating a cell phone... Alien's need humans to worship them, for simpler channeling into people SOUL, to control their fate.

Microdeception

I Ponder if these QUANTUM ENGINEERING BEINGS, utilizing a TUBE Technology, have also Accomplished Longevity by making Perplex Essential Environments in Protoplanets? If True, I strongly believe that these cleverer Extraterrestrials are living unthinkable Ages!

I suspect the same Alien Beings, Possessing Human Livelihoods 5,500 years ago, are still viewing us now! We can Achieve Longevity too, but as we get Older, we'll decrease in Stature, and our Skin could look like Elephants, as the Human Body Modify to Deep Time.

Achieving Longevity, maybe Human's Easiest Quest. However, Living without our Splendor Looks, Agility, along with Pleasure, while seeing Agile Beings Dying soon, but Enjoying Tastier Foods and Entertainment, would also be unbearable, for Humankind, overtime.

Consequently, TUBE Raptures Achieved by Creating Assimilated Worlds are crucial to ease a Solitary Life. But it seems the Enemy (Aliens) doesn't want to see us as Rivals, and a Sinister Script has been Written in the Bible Religion Book, which is beyond Epic indeed.

The BYE-BOWL (BIBLE) Predicts the last Battle of our fiery demise, and it can happen by Nuclear Weapons aimed at all Continents now! This maybe Alien God's last Tempt-salute, but Bunkers are set up for some to Survive, and Restart CON Civilizations all over again.

THE NUCLEAR BLITZKRIEG!

CIVILIZATIONS RISEN 5500 YEARS AGO, BUT HUMAN'S PLANE ENDEAVORS WERE THE SAME UNTIL AROUND 200 YEARS AGO; WHEN WE SUDDENLY HAD GENIUSES FARADAY, MENDELEEV, & EINSTEIN LOGGING OPTIC IMAGES FROM BAD ALIENS THAT PROPELLED OTHERS TO BUILD MAD HYDROGEN NUCLEAR BOMBS. SO, WE BEEN SET UP FOLKS! NOW THIS WEAPONRY WILL BE UTILIZED AS A NEFARIOUS DETERRENT TO HALT OUR INDEPENDENCE AIMED BY FREE THINKING HUMANS.

By Darian Vernon Graves.

NUCLEAR =INSIDE-YOU-CLEAR, and people made Alien's more Powerful by Exploding Alpha Particle Bombs inside our Atmosphere, during the Cold War.

Nuclear Power Plants are Schemed to Fail from our Mistakes and Earthquakes, to excel Alpha Particles in the Atmosphere daily. Aliens pick Oppressors, to lead Nations, and Bribe folks that persist Abrasions.

How is this CON possible? Well, clever Alien Gods, TUBE Live, works likened to Mobile Electronics that, chiefly, need the top 3 Super Electrical Conductive Elements Silver, Copper, or Gold to work elite today.

But remove these 3 Metals inside Cellular Phones? The Capabilities, Band Width Bars are Diminished, and it makes them Inept or Useless. So, eliminating exposure to Super EC Elements and Alpha Particles, should chiefly Liberate folks from Micro-deception.

How do Extraterrestrial God's, Living in Deep Space, reach us? Imagine Humanity Utilizing Dark Matter Energy, to quickly reach the Universe Borders, and Communicate with other Beings in Space; without leaving Folks Dominion, like Earth Satellite Phones.

However, if they're Primitive and Utilizing Natural things, like our Ancestors desired in Africa 40,000 years ago, Human Live Reception would be modest.

Alien's Implemented Invasive Deceptions to reach us daily. Blood and Red Ochre contains the seventh most EC Element Iron (EC 17%), which is still utilized.

BEER =BE-ER

In Ice Age Europe, about 39,300 years ago, a Spirit of an Obese Woman, was Marketed by Venus Figurines; these Spirits were likely Extraterrestrial Virgin Mary's, that are still known to Help lost people, in need, now.

Obesity Influenced People to Slaughter and Eat Large Mammals, about 39,300 years ago; using Red Ochre risen around the same time. After a Comet Explosion, 26,500 years later, Blood Rituals at Altars were often Aliens most exploited things for Human Beings to do.

BREW =BE-OUR-EW. Oxygen Rust Iron. So, folk were misled by Alien God's to make Beer with Pottery, that contains Aluminum, for increasing Reception in users.

Brewing BE-ER (BEER) and Cooking Foods, in Pottery, frequently leached Super EC Aluminum inside Human Beings Daily Meals; this everlasting Metals Corrosion Resistance, also increased Alien God's Live Reception inside people, over Blood Rituals, which persist daily.

Around 5,000 BCE, Turquoise was utilized as, "Chakra Stones" because it contains large amounts of Copper and Aluminum. Moreover, these two Elements are the second and fourth most Electro-Conductivity Metals.

Furthermore, Copper and Aluminum were also widely chosen because there's over a 50% drop, in Electrical Conductivity, to fifth most EC Element Zinc (EC 27%).

Microdeception

Compared to Aluminum, Copper (Atomic #29) is a, substantially, superior Electrical Conductive Element, because Aluminum (Atomic #13) is lighter; this could be seen by changing weak Aluminum (EC 61%) Video Jacks to the higher output Copper (EC 100%) on a TV.

Super EC Silver, Gold, and Copper also made it much easier for Aliens to seize our Souls, like downloading Movies. Moreover, billions of people are also Buried inside 6 feet Graves, Globally, because Bones contain our Life Highlights, in Video and Sound, called SOUL.

Atoms and Human's DNA sendoff Signature Signals, that my evidence suggests are being downloaded by a Quantum Technology now. Extraterrestrials, belied as Gods, achieved this CON from offering numerous Myths of Immortality, that persist to Humans today.

BELIED =BE-LIED. Aliens are watching us, likened to Satellite TV, and we're producing Live Entertainment 24/7. Sadly, people are being duped, from Religions, & preparing for Afterlife Experiences we call Heaven.

Sorry folks, Heaven is also a CON, caused by Alien's Marketing Simulated Worlds; this started from Vivid Near Death Experiences, appearing as beloved Dead people living inside Paradise, that folk, unknowingly, still market to millions of Humans Worldwide today.

LIVED = DEVIL

PRAISE =PEE-RAISE, and my Evidence Suggest these are Simulated Worlds, that chiefly works by utilizing our 7 chakras; this Technology is Victorious and 100 times more Gratifying, than Folks Pitiful Lives, today.

Perplex Simulated Worlds, Implemented by Human seven Chakras (Glands) Looks, Smells, and Feels Real! So, these clever Beings could experience all our Vivid Encounters Live, and Enhance the Pleasures without Harm being caused to Aliens Body. But we always do!

Consequently, Aliens are using Control Elements like Fuel. So, Silver, Gold, and Copper were often insisted for Jewelry; this also made the first KINGDOMS, and it's a Homophone word, which signifies KING-DUMB.

For Religious Folks Programmed to BE-OXEN (BOX), & can't Insight God CON? Rival beings want our Soul for Fun, and this is expected from the LIVED (DEVIL).

Nomadic Humanity Lived Righteously, but it's boring to watch. So, Aliens Created Barbaric Civilizations for Strife, Plunder, Toiling, Prostitution, Slavery, Debt, & BE-ER (BEER) for Persuading Domestic Violence daily.

Preserving Extraterrestrial's Dark Reception, by Pure Control Elements, was a Priority. So, tons of Copper, Gold, and Silver were Mined from using Slave Labor. Occasionally, Aliens would allow Workers FREEDOM (FREE-DUMB) for Emotional Entertainment Displays.

Extraterrestrial God's insisted Languages, Religions, & Customs Everywhere the Control Elements was used. Sadly, Humankind is still deceived by this CON, which divided folks with Prejudice and sustained Five Races.

Since the Birth of Civilization, Clothing has been Key, because it's like Simulation Suits Making Movies, and these Ethnic Costumes also DATE THE AGES OF MEN, for enduring Cruel Beings in the Cosmos Amusement.

Sun UV Rays make Vitamin D, and can push Control Elements out of People Bodies rapidly. So, preserving these Metals in folks, was achieved by moving bigger Kingdoms further away from Earth Tropics (Equator).

Sadly, it still deprives billions of people, Good Health, today. Super Conductive Gold also makes it easier to Steal Human Beings Dramatic Souls, which are stored inside Folk Bones, and contain people Life Highlights.

Alien God's Downloads our Souls, like Software daily, and Create Perplex Simulated Worlds, Deities Termed Heaven. Gold is superior at retrieving Souls. So, folks burying Bodies inside Homes and Towers like Jericho, in Neolithic Times by using Iron Ochre, were obsolete.

It seems the first Civilizations risen in Sumer, Ta-Seti, and Kemet Deserts for Saving People Soul with Gold. In-fact, these same larger Burial Mounds, are also still preserving Skeletons in Iraq, Sudan, and Egypt today.

MICRODECEPTION

Why Humankind Buries the Deceased? The Neolithic Age had Sculptors and House Paintings of Vultures Devouring Bodies in the Elements. Alien's Marketed this to Scare us, into Burying our Dead, for Paradise in their Afterlife. But it's Histories biggest Deception.

Humans DNA sendoff Signature Signals, 24/7, and Clever Six Feet Deep Graves are chiefly Designed to Protect our Bodies Life Highlights; this, supposedly, come in two parts called SOUL (VIDEO and SOUND).

The Body Decomposes rapidly in the Elements, and Prolong Exposure to Sun Rays should eradicate our SOULS itself. So, Deity Burials are still utilized today.

But the last thing we should do, is Bury our Bodies, because Quantum Engineering should soon make it easier for Hackers to Download SOULS when people are Alive too! Additionally, Droplets, Dust, and our Children could also carry Human SOULS, from DNA.

Ancient Cities Garbage, Stockyards, and Graveyards were also Poisonous to People Health; this Pollution released Nitrogen Dioxide, Methane, and Ammonia.

Today, Kemet Mummy Lungs are looking like Heavy Smokers, because Humans were Living on a Smelly Landfill every day. So, Perilous Incense Smoke was Burning often, to Freshen Up Bad Air Pollution daily.

Smelting Rocks for Raw Metals also caused Harm to their Bodies. Sadly, people still do this, Globally, and are Programmed to disregard their Health for CASH.

Kemet

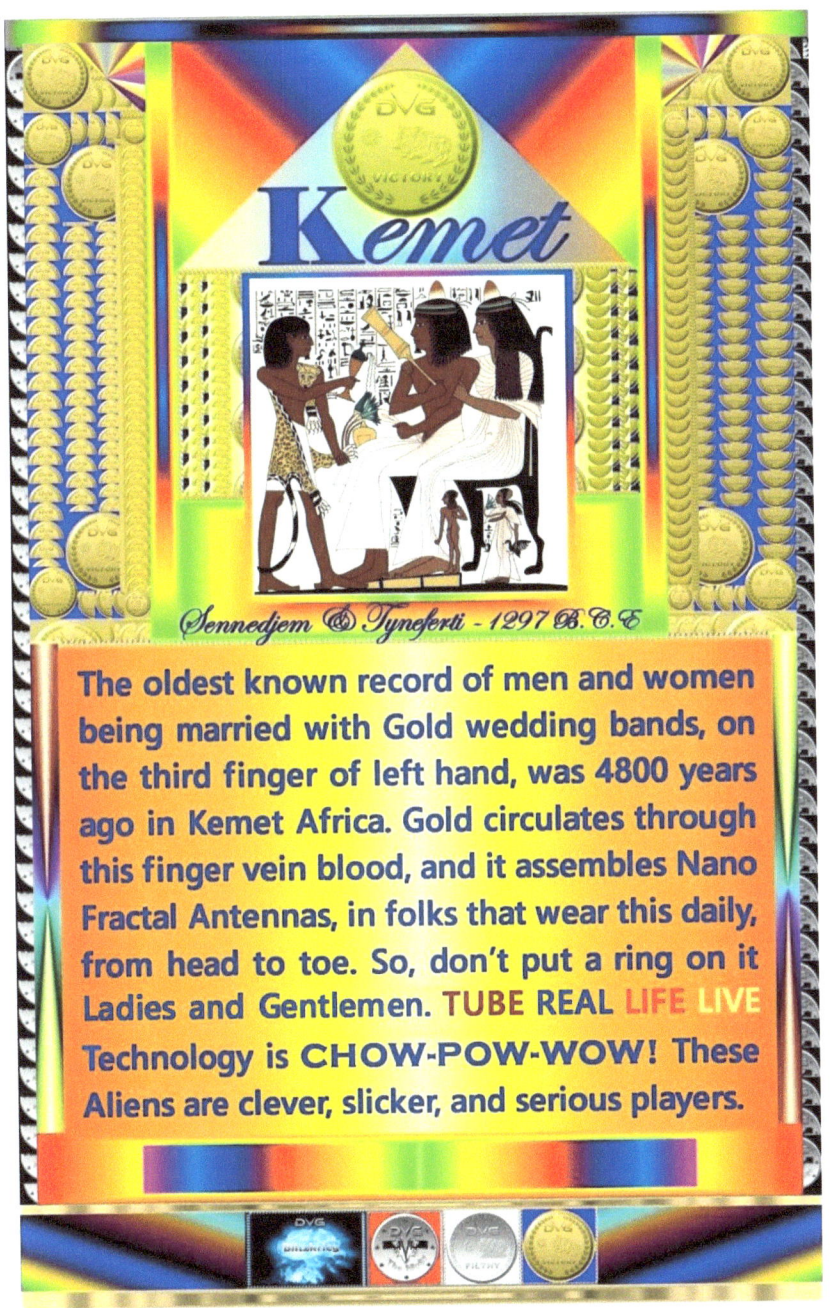

Sennedjem & Tyneferti - 1297 B.C.E

The oldest known record of men and women being married with Gold wedding bands, on the third finger of left hand, was 4800 years ago in Kemet Africa. Gold circulates through this finger vein blood, and it assembles Nano Fractal Antennas, in folks that wear this daily, from head to toe. So, don't put a ring on it Ladies and Gentlemen. TUBE REAL LIFE LIVE Technology is CHOW-POW-WOW! These Aliens are clever, slicker, and serious players.

KHUFU & KHAFRE

THE SLICK (GREAT) PYRAMID OF GIZA was, supposedly, built for King Khufu's Tomb and folks toiled like Ants to erect it. But they were conned; this is mostly a huge Fractal Antenna, likened to WI-FI ROUTERS in Cities, but this Technology gave Alien's ubiquity to ROUT inside us! Creepy, this bleak Monument was also conspired to Tempt Humankind, and its CONDUCTIVITY DISCONTINUITY is still the highest, in this Cairo Region, today.

DEODERANT =DE-ODER-ANT, and we mostly Apply Aluminum under People Armpits; this is making an EC Base like Cellular Phone Frames.

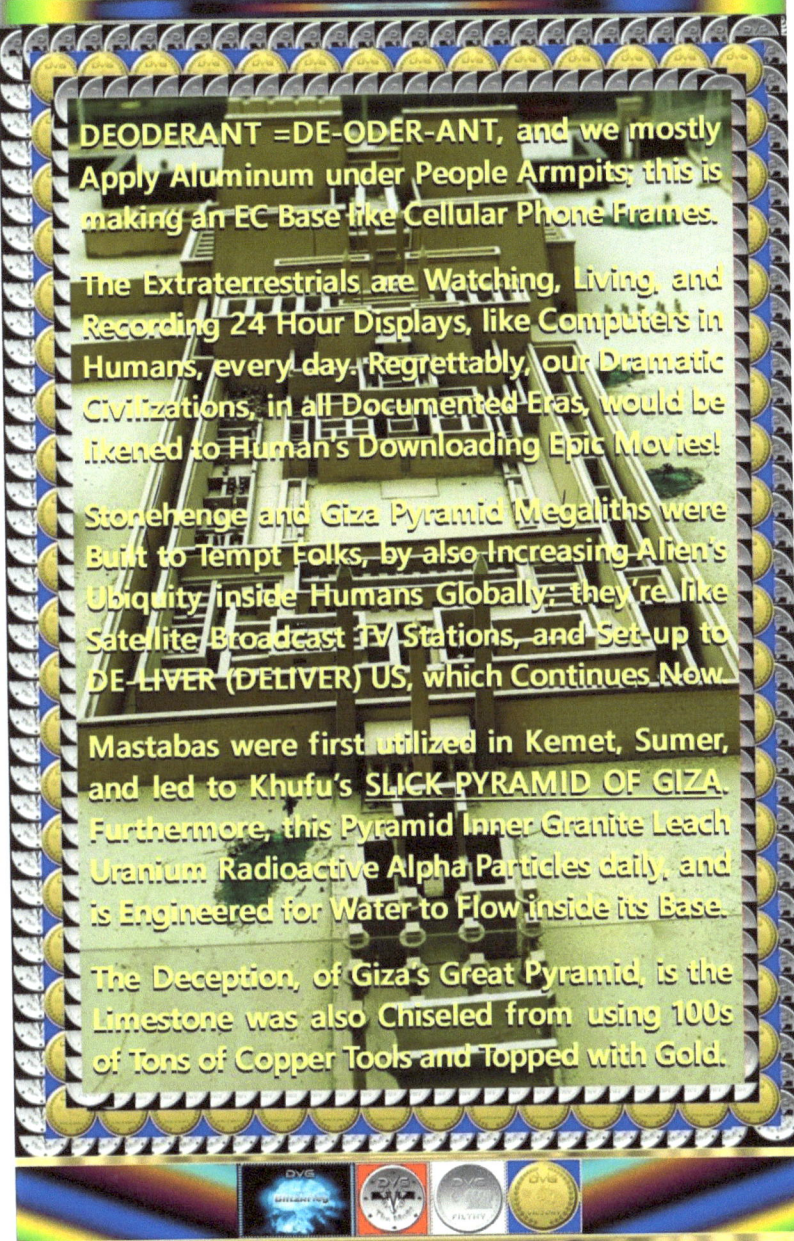

The Extraterrestrials are Watching, Living, and Recording 24 Hour Displays, like Computers in Humans, every day. Regrettably, our Dramatic Civilizations, in all Documented Eras, would be likened to Human's Downloading Epic Movies!

Stonehenge and Giza Pyramid Megaliths were Built to Tempt Folks, by also Increasing Alien's Ubiquity inside Humans Globally; they're like Satellite Broadcast TV Stations, and Set-up to DE-LIVER (DELIVER) US, which Continues Now.

Mastabas were first utilized in Kemet, Sumer, and led to Khufu's SLICK PYRAMID OF GIZA. Furthermore, this Pyramid Inner Granite Leach Uranium Radioactive Alpha Particles daily, and is Engineered for Water to Flow inside its Base.

The Deception, of Giza's Great Pyramid, is the Limestone was also Chiseled from using 100s of Tons of Copper Tools and Topped with Gold.

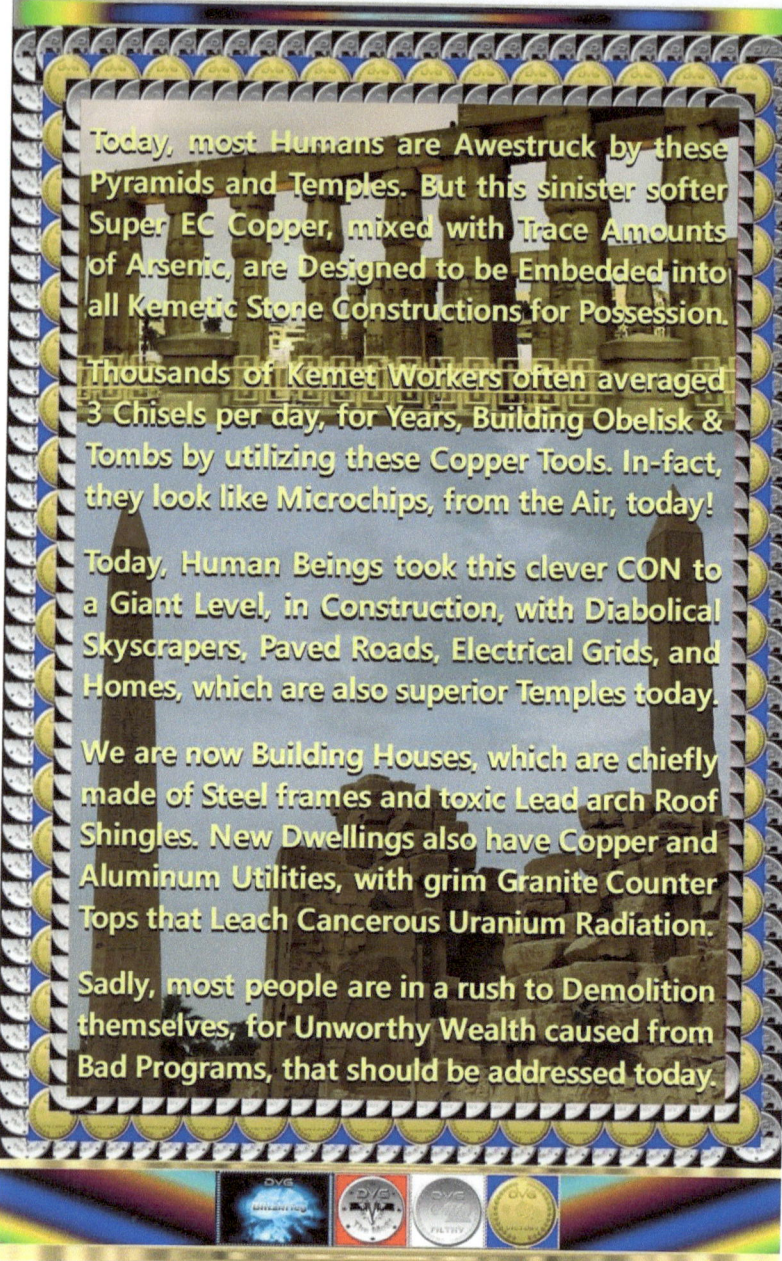

Today, most Humans are Awestruck by these Pyramids and Temples. But this sinister softer Super EC Copper, mixed with Trace Amounts of Arsenic, are Designed to be Embedded into all Kemetic Stone Constructions for Possession.

Thousands of Kemet Workers often averaged 3 Chisels per day, for Years, Building Obelisk & Tombs by utilizing these Copper Tools. In-fact, they look like Microchips, from the Air, today!

Today, Human Beings took this clever CON to a Giant Level, in Construction, with Diabolical Skyscrapers, Paved Roads, Electrical Grids, and Homes, which are also superior Temples today.

We are now Building Houses, which are chiefly made of Steel frames and toxic Lead arch Roof Shingles. New Dwellings also have Copper and Aluminum Utilities, with grim Granite Counter Tops that Leach Cancerous Uranium Radiation.

Sadly, most people are in a rush to Demolition themselves, for Unworthy Wealth caused from Bad Programs, that should be addressed today.

Persistence

Aliens are staging People Oppressions, 24/7, by also Bribing World Leaders with Luxuries, Exotic Concubines, and CASH. But Control Elements & Religions Prolong Alien God's PLAY-NETWORK.

Historically, Extraterrestrial God's utilized Orbs to switch into other Beings, they're likely also Possessing, in the Universe. Alien's Chief God is an Assimilated Quantum Android called Amun, who has ubiquity from Gold and Temples today.

It is written that Aliens are from Constellations in Space. So, we may never know who they are or where they're living in our Massive Universe.

Noteworthy, they're numerous people that call them the Grays. So, it seems Human Beings are Buried in termed GRAVES, for Soul, because it's an Abbreviation of Aliens called GRAY-VIDEOS?

TODAY, PEOPLE ON THE PLAY-NETWORK HAVE NO CLUE THEY'RE BEING WHIZ BY DEVIOUS ALIEN GODS FOR DISPLAY; THIS IS A HUGE DIFFERENCE FROM SUMERIAN AND KEMET TIMES WHO ALSO DOCUMENTED THESE BIZARRE GRATIFICATIONS.

Persistence

SEE-ON (CON) is thriving, and we'll likely never know who our Alien Oppressors are. But what uses Antenna's to Transmit, lives underground, & is The Most Successful Species on our Planet?

Yes, the Insect is more likely than a Mammal to Persevere, during Natural Disasters, and Perfect this Technology. So, Perplex Simulated World's (TUBE), which Human Beings are still Misled to call Heaven, could be the Insect Creation today.

GENIUS =GENIE-US. Worshipers are Online with Alien's Mentally daily. Human Unruly Trends for Kingdoms, Entertainment, Education, Style, and Humanities Newer Defraud Constitutions were all Downloaded, like a Computer App, for Show.

Great Creators are termed Genius, and were also SHOW-SIN (CHOSEN) for the Diabolical WHIZ-DUMB (WISDOM), which brought Cruel Wealth.

Many past Geniuses Slept with a Pen and Paper, to Record their inner Alien God Downloads, that chiefly caused us more Mischief, which persists.

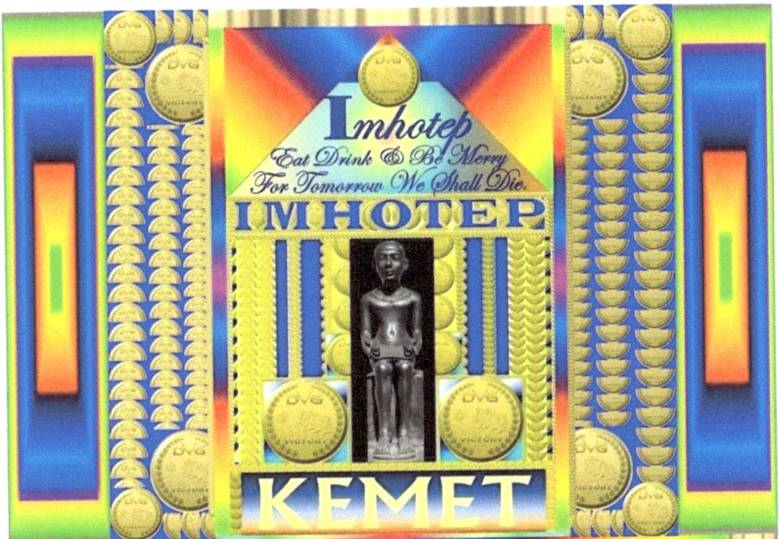

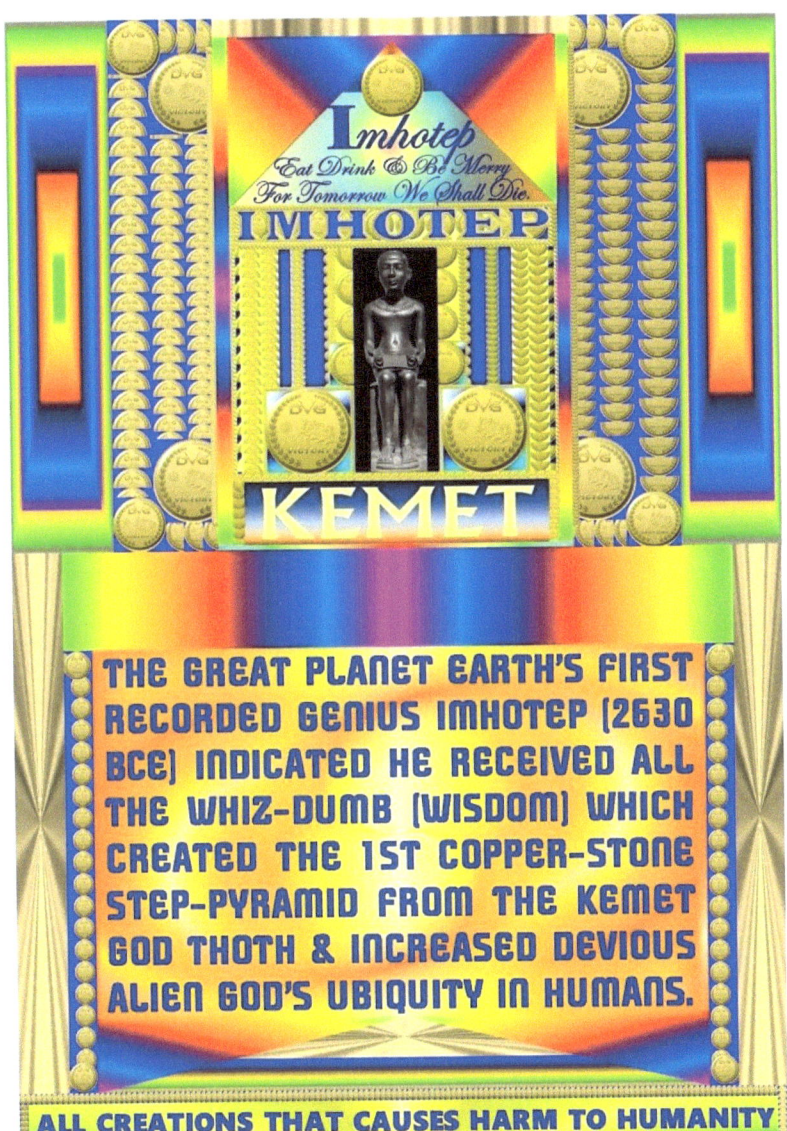

THE GREAT PLANET EARTH'S FIRST RECORDED GENIUS IMHOTEP (2630 BCE) INDICATED HE RECEIVED ALL THE WHIZ-DUMB (WISDOM) WHICH CREATED THE 1ST COPPER-STONE STEP-PYRAMID FROM THE KEMET GOD THOTH & INCREASED DEVIOUS ALIEN GOD'S UBIQUITY IN HUMANS.

ALL CREATIONS THAT CAUSES HARM TO HUMANITY HEALTH ARE WHIZ-DUMB (WISDOM) AND THE HIGH PRIEST IMHOTEP REALIZED THIS, DURING HIS LATER YEARS, WHO ALSO SEEMED TO HAVE REGRETS IN LIFE.

Albert Einstein (1879-1955) was a great scientist and also a remarkable philosopher of peace. He said "behind everything there is an order, by this since, I am a religious man." "We know nothing about God and the World at all. All our knowledge is but the knowledge of school children. Possible, we shall know a little more than we do now. But the real nature of things we shall never know, never." "The concept of a soul without a body seems to me to be empty and devoid of meaning." "That a man can take pleasure in marching, in formation, to the strings of a band, is enough to make me despised him. He has only been given his big brain by mistake; a backbone was all he needed. This plague spots of Civilization ought to be abolish with all possible speed (I agree)." Hydrogen Nuclear Weapons (H-bomb 1955). "Stark and dreadful and inescapable: Shall we put an end of the Human race, or shall Mankind renounce War?" "(1949) The world is a dangerous place to live; not because of the people who are evil, but because of the people who don't do anything about it.-Albert Einstein

Is there a heaven? Yes, you're living on a miracle planet that's perfect for you 24/7. Is there a hell? Yes, if you commit a crime that leads you to jail, and the suicide bombers that were offered seventy virgins in paradise after death, for blowing up the New York World Trade Center on 09/11/2001, are unfortunately done having fun for eternity. Human life can last a very long time and there's nothing to fear but accidents, illnesses, or seeing our love ones dying while living here. However, our instincts make seeing or hearing them again true, for no vision, sound, or smell can be loss in heavy atoms too (soul) and these are quantum mechanics making vivid dreams (simulation) inside you.

Life

is wonderful,

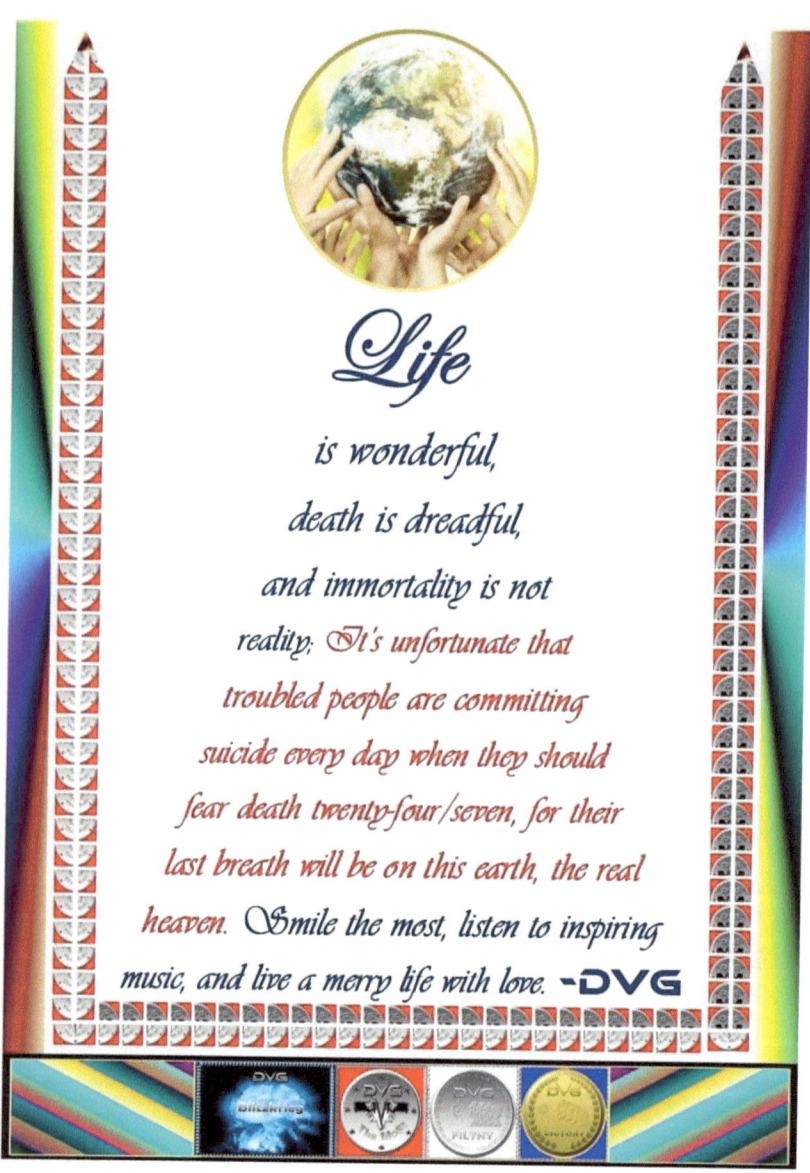

death is dreadful,

and immortality is not

reality; It's unfortunate that

troubled people are committing

suicide every day when they should

fear death twenty-four/seven, for their

last breath will be on this earth, the real

heaven. Smile the most, listen to inspiring

music, and live a merry life with love. -DVG

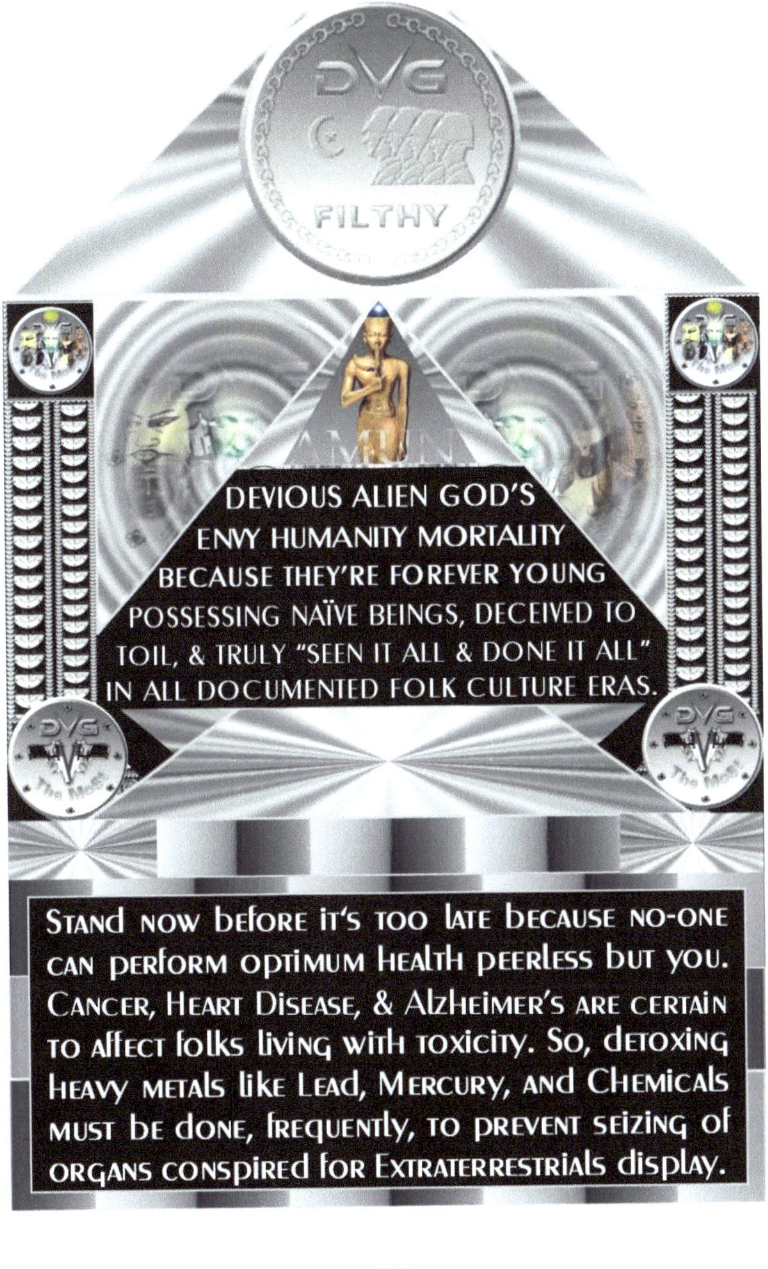
DVG
FILTHY
DEVIOUS ALIEN GOD'S
ENVY HUMANITY MORTALITY
BECAUSE THEY'RE FOREVER YOUNG
POSSESSING NAÏVE BEINGS, DECEIVED TO
TOIL, & TRULY "SEEN IT ALL & DONE IT ALL"
IN ALL DOCUMENTED FOLK CULTURE ERAS.
Stand now before it's too late because no-one
can perform optimum health peerless but you.
Cancer, Heart Disease, & Alzheimer's are certain
to affect folks living with toxicity. So, detoxing
heavy metals like Lead, Mercury, and Chemicals
must be done, frequently, to prevent seizing of
organs conspired for Extraterrestrials display.

The #1 Deception, in Human Documented History, is the Afterlife, and they're still Produced, in numerous Simulated Worlds, for Deceiving Human Beings daily.

Believing in Paradise, after People Passing, made us Careless and Unafraid of Death; this caused Rampant Suicides, the Tragic Burying of Humans Alive, and a vicious cycle of Bloody Wars for Alien God's Pleasure.

Angels and Demons are some of Humankind's Most Documented Encounters in History. But this a CON, executed by a Technology, I termed The Hidden One.

My Overall Evidence Suggests they're Carbon Orbs, using Trace Amounts of Super Electrical Conductive Element's, and can also Transfer into any Simulated Visual Object, that's Loaded inside Alien's Game App.

The Hidden One Sphere's, chiefly, utilize the Thermal Conductive Element Carbon, because it has 4 Bonds (Outer Electrons), which Diamonds are also made of.

Human Beings Logged Demons since Ancient Times, and they have Extraordinary Stellar Powers. So, don't Tempt them today, for they could cause Swift Death!

Alien's also Produced Killer Cold Haunted Houses by using Demonic Possession. I suspect this was caused by Chilling Bodies, like we can do with Copper inside a Freezer, to remake Carbon into a Stronger Carbyne. But they utilize Copper inside our Chakras and Veins.

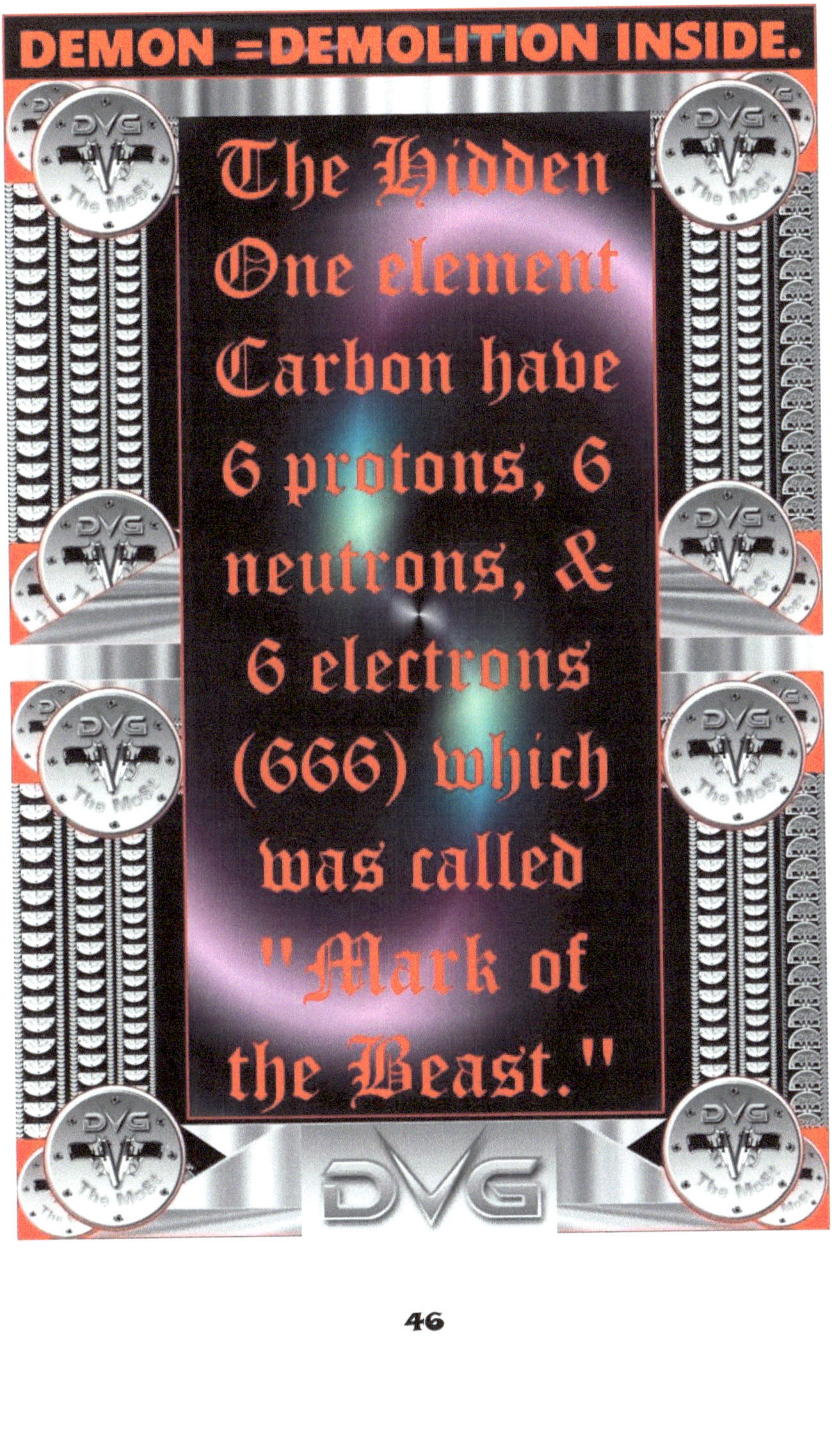
DEMON =DEMOLITION INSIDE.
The Hidden One element Carbon have 6 protons, 6 neutrons, & 6 electrons (666) which was called "Mark of the Beast."
DVG
The Most

AWARD =A-WARD.

HAUNTED =HUNTED US, and Demons are being used to enforce Aliens will over World Leader's by pressing them into Warfare's for, supposedly, Peace. But Scaring People are TUBE Pleasures, and Haunted House Ghost Market Heavens; this is pivotal to prolong Alien's CON.

Historically, Gold, Silver, and Bronze (Copper/Tin) were given away as Honorary Metals at War. Today, it's also Sports, Movies, Music, and Honor for Peace, Humans call "The Nobel Prize," is made from 18-23 Karat Gold. So, disregard Toiling your Body for A-WARD (AWARD).

Deities Can Allure Humans Wearing These Metals. So, I now call them Shining Death! Regrettably, most folks don't realize they're being turned up, like Transistors, by Control Elements in Dwellings, Cookware, Jewelry, Transports, Makeup, and People EC Clothing every day.

CIVILIZATION IS AN EXTRATERRESTRIAL ART OF DECEIT, and People are being Programmed, by Amoral Codes, to push all Phases of their Livelihoods to the Breaking point, for prolonging numerous Alien Clever Raptures.

PAID =PEE-AID, and people form PLOTS (PEE-LOTS) to get Cash from a CON or Murder, but don't ask WHY? Humans do their Jobs, get Paid, and Lose it by taking a Stand, Knee, or Speaking up against the Evil Recurring.

Moreover, Humankind biggest problem is Desecrating Itself, and not Demonic Programs Causing Harm daily. So, BE-RIGHT (BRIGHT), and avoid Alien's Bait Luxuries.

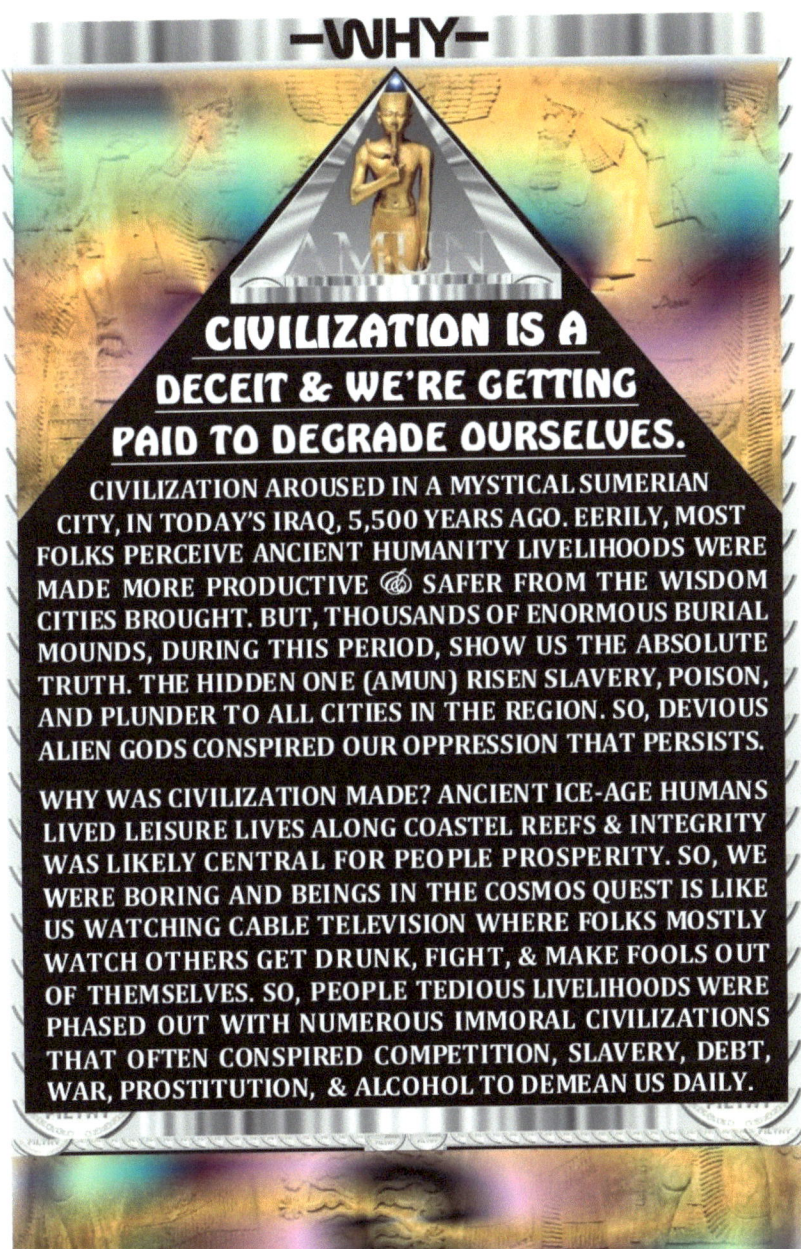

CIVILIZATION IS A DECEIT & WE'RE GETTING PAID TO DEGRADE OURSELVES.

CIVILIZATION AROUSED IN A MYSTICAL SUMERIAN CITY, IN TODAY'S IRAQ, 5,500 YEARS AGO. EERILY, MOST FOLKS PERCEIVE ANCIENT HUMANITY LIVELIHOODS WERE MADE MORE PRODUCTIVE & SAFER FROM THE WISDOM CITIES BROUGHT. BUT, THOUSANDS OF ENORMOUS BURIAL MOUNDS, DURING THIS PERIOD, SHOW US THE ABSOLUTE TRUTH. THE HIDDEN ONE (AMUN) RISEN SLAVERY, POISON, AND PLUNDER TO ALL CITIES IN THE REGION. SO, DEVIOUS ALIEN GODS CONSPIRED OUR OPPRESSION THAT PERSISTS.

WHY WAS CIVILIZATION MADE? ANCIENT ICE-AGE HUMANS LIVED LEISURE LIVES ALONG COASTEL REEFS & INTEGRITY WAS LIKELY CENTRAL FOR PEOPLE PROSPERITY. SO, WE WERE BORING AND BEINGS IN THE COSMOS QUEST IS LIKE US WATCHING CABLE TELEVISION WHERE FOLKS MOSTLY WATCH OTHERS GET DRUNK, FIGHT, & MAKE FOOLS OUT OF THEMSELVES. SO, PEOPLE TEDIOUS LIVELIHOODS WERE PHASED OUT WITH NUMEROUS IMMORAL CIVILIZATIONS THAT OFTEN CONSPIRED COMPETITION, SLAVERY, DEBT, WAR, PROSTITUTION, & ALCOHOL TO DEMEAN US DAILY.

Archaeologists located statues of Osiris in Abydos Egypt; in myth, his wife Isis (Auset), who's also this man's sister, helped Osiris resurrect from a tragic death caused by an evil brother name Set (Sutekh).

The cleverer God Ausar (Osiris) is Anubis father; he was, supposedly, Kemet's first King, from the Star Sirius, and was chiefly painted green for creating Agriculture that made Human Civilization possible.

BE-ER (BEER) was also 1st produced by Ausar and he marketed how to make it around the whole Fertile Crescent. Alien Gods setup people with Agriculture because this toiling work, perilous Wheat Lectins, leaching Heavy Metal Cookware, and consumption of Alcohol still reduces Humanity average Lifespan.

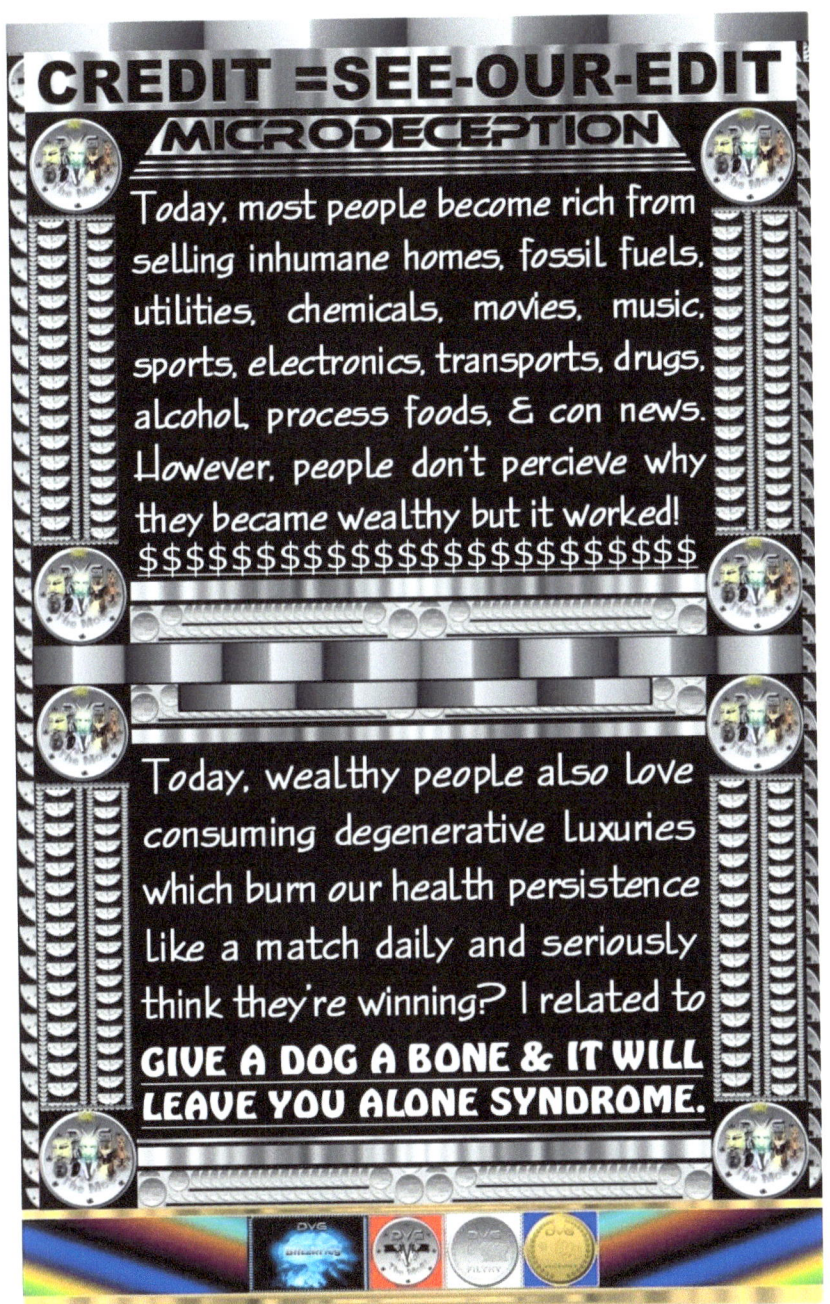

CREDIT =SEE-OUR-EDIT

MICRODECEPTION

Today, most people become rich from selling inhumane homes, fossil fuels, utilities, chemicals, movies, music, sports, electronics, transports, drugs, alcohol, process foods, & con news. However, people don't percieve why they became wealthy but it worked!

$$$$$$$$$$$$$$$$$$$$$$$$$$$$

Today, wealthy people also love consuming degenerative luxuries which burn our health persistence like a match daily and seriously think they're winning? I related to **GIVE A DOG A BONE & IT WILL LEAVE YOU ALONE SYNDROME.**

Historically,
the more people
toil workers,
sell perilous
stock, hustle &
influence trends
that degrade
livelihoods;
the wealthier
The Hidden
One made them.
DVG

BLEACH =BE-LEACH.

PAIN =PEE-A-INSIDE. A Human Being takes around 20,000 Breaths and consume 35 pounds of Air daily. So, Cities are constructed, with Permanent Dwellings, to DE-WELL (DWELL) Humankind's Health every day.

Most folks consume tons of Bad Air mixed with Dust, Heavier Elements, and Chemicals from Paints yearly, because Alien's like to SEE-OUR-EDIT (CREDIT) daily!

Kemetics made Clothing out of Linen (Flax). But they were insisted, by Deities, to Bleach them White daily in Aluminum Sulfates, which Children, under the age of Six, were Banned to Wear. Likely, because Parents Logged its Toxicity Symptoms to their Babies Health.

Although, this Element has always been known to be Toxic, and also why Atomic #13 (Aluminum) is still a very Bad number today. Historically, People Youthful Encounters were desired by Extraterrestrials Globally.

BLEACH =BE-LEACH, by foul Detergents, Cookware, Transports, Paints, Clothing, and Hygiene Byproducts for SHORTENING (BUTTER) Humanity Lifespan, why?

POISONOUS =POISON-US, because we can achieve Longevity. Note, Human DNA also confirms we were Childbearing at much older Ages too, before Africa's Neolithic. So, Alien God's are driven to dispose Elders and Prize the Most Exquisite Encounters from Youth.

BREAD =BE-READ. Feeling Uncomfortable? Well, you could be Eating Poison, three times daily, because our DAILY BREAD is also Laced with EC Elements for Show.

TIN =TEN, because it needs 10% Tin and 90% Copper to make Bronze (TIN -Atomic #50 EC is 15%). Mining EC Elements and Grinding Grains for Bread were the most Toiling work, people did, during Sumerian times.

Alien God's insisted they make their Bread using Oval Pans of Bronze, into Pancakes, which Leached Larger Amounts of Pure Copper and Tin Poison in their Food.

Human Bodies can remove Bad Foods from the Colon and Skin. However, not large quantities of Pure Metals which chiefly settles in People Organs and Bones daily.

COOKWARE (COOKWEAR), SILVERWARE (SILVERWEAR). People can measure Metal, being leached inside Food, by doing an "Alkaline Baking Soda Test." But don't try this utilizing toxic Teflon Cookware; this could kill you.

The first Attire was also made to Increase Alien's Live Reception from Bleaching them in Aluminum Sulfates. BAKE =BE-ACHE, and we're Naive to God Scams. But Humankind can turn the corner by consuming Natural Items as our Ancestors did, in Africa, 40,000 years ago.

Sadly, People Living Leisurely and Achieving Longevity would, certainly, be Alien God's Nightmare. So, we're being influenced for Toiling, Competing, and Warring inside Civilization, to perpetuate this PLAY-NETWORK.

"Do our World Leaders know what's really happening to us today?" Historically, 99% of Human Superiors were chosen, because they Worshiped Alien's and didn't know it. But they didn't make us "Crash Dummies," for 5500 Betraying years, by just a Deceit.

Ancient Priest Kings, like China's Emperor Ch'in (Qin Shi Huang 259–210 BCE), which did realize Humans were being Duped by Perplex Simulated Heavens, and Inquired Others How to Achieve Immortality? They were often Trounced, by a Demonic Force!

Ch'in was misguided to consume Mercury, from Demons, and this Killed him quickly. So, Demonic Oppressions by Alien Hidden Enforcers were often Hostile, and Insisted all Leaders to do whatever Cruelties, Alien Gods desired, for the Kings Peace at Night.

Demonic Oppression and Possession were made possible from Kings ingesting Super EC Elements; found inside Gold Cookware, Silver Drinking Vessels, Jewellery, Crowns, or Monatomic Gold Elixir Cones, produced from Bread, which was called SHO-BREAD.

Mercury (Atomic #80) is an Very Bad Liquid Metal and Top Ten EC Element. Some Doctors say, it can be Healthy for us by averting Diseases, but this a CON.

Mercury is a Toxic Heavy Metal, and all Microorganisms will soon be screened from Humans utilizing Smart Detectors.

Furthermore, there's no ultimate healer than the Human Immune System, that's a Persistent Fighting Machine when it's not Poisoned from Heavy Elements and Chemicals delivered by Bad Alien God's.

Cleverly, Mercury is also used in Animal Vaccines to Leach in Meat, Humans Eat, for Increasing Alien's Reception in folks.

VACCINE =VACCUM-SCENE, and clever Mercury is picked, because it Flows like a Snake. So, it's now being Misused to Increase Microdeception in Humankind and Failing Organs, which also leads to Surgery, that's an Ill Demolition Display.

Homophones are, frequently, DROLL (LORD) Meanings, which sounds the same as Words like KETCHUP =CATCH-UP. Although, this is often what it signifies Ladies and Gentlemen.

Ketchup is mostly made from Tomatoes and Lethal Vinegar Acid, which I'll explain later. The Tomato Contains Lectin Proteins, Plants adapted this, as defenses, inside other Foods like Wheat to also prevent from being Eaten.

Lectins Can Kill Insects Fast, and often cause "Leaky Gut Syndrome" inside us! So, Human Beings really should CATCH-UP (KETCHUP), to this deception, for optimum Health today.

MADAM and DEIFIED are Palindrome words. The Obese MADAM Figurine is our Earliest Known God, and was Worshiped by Humans for over 25,000 years. It seems she ruled like a Queen Bee, in Ancient Times, but likened to a Computer DAM (MAD) that halted folks.

Males were later chosen to be Kings, during the Birth of Human Civilization, 5,500 years ago. The Sumerian Tablets, that archived the first EC Attire worn by Adam and Eve, are a Foremost Archaeological Discovery. But this is Hindered for Sustaining Monotheism now.

CLOVER =SEE-LOVER. Younger Women are Chosen to Birth too many Babies, which is Bad for Health, & they're more Oppressed for Dividing Human Beings.

The Electrical Grid, with Copper Wires surrounding people, made Alien's more Powerful on Earth than ever. So, Democracies and Constitutions CON for a Profit with LAWS (WALL) Designed to Oppress, why?

DOG-PEE-POLES (GOD PEOPLES) ARE BE-OXEN (BOX), & no-longer Control their Fate, to see they're being Scammed by God's daily. Historically, Toiling, Debt, and Alcohol kept most people in line, which persists.

Human Independence could be achieved. But most people are Programmed by Amoral Codes to Deceit and cause Harm to others or relinquish the Luxuries.

Alien God's can Possess all Life and implement Racial Programs, against Different Ethnics, to keep people dissociated like a Dog Breed, for Live Entertainment.

Moreover, this is a Sinister Agenda today. Different Ethnics, Conceiving Children, are also likened to the Mutt Dogs being Born with lesser Genetic Disorders.

I suspect most Races have Separate Programs, that causes many Unique Trends in Folks Clothing, Food Preferences, Customs, and this seems simple. People are Driven to do the things, which makes them Feel Good by increasing their DOPAMINE (DOPE-A-MEN).

Today, it seems Controlling other Ethnic's Fate, from Interbreeding Couples Children, could be Diminished when Assorted in more Racial Combinations, because this may Delay Alien Programs and Prompt Schemes.

Consequently, Mixed Babies are a Bigger Problem to Aliens, and likely Crucial to Humanity Independence, from Extraterrestrial God's PLAY-NETWORK, by being likened to us utilizing a Deactivated Cell Phone today.

Sadly, the Pharaohs of Kemet, were insisted to Marry Sisters for Causing Epilepsy and Congenital Disorders to Deprive their Kids. These Incest Diseases Increased Alien God's Live Reception, in Offspring many times, & also Created more Races during The Neolithic Age.

Aliens Regulator Despised Interbreeding People and made Fierce Prejudice Programs that made Humanity MORE-ON (MORON) which also caused Bloody Wars.

Regrettably, it's still making Crash Dummies out of us daily, and Strife shouldn't recur to Beings with our Intelligence. So, we should Insight Steps to Abolish it.

Kemet God HORUS =WHORE-US, and JESUS name is Pronounced JEEZ-US. But folks still Pronounce their God Names, repeatedly, for Alien's Comedic Pleasure.

PRAY =PREY, and it's Pronounced the same, because Humans are Prey when Praying to God's, that Possess us. PRAY also means PEE-RAY, and this can be seen in the Praying Groups Quantum Entanglement Particles.

SCRIPTURE =SCRIPT, and Sham Religions, that Stage Wars, are going to Destroy us, if Humans don't realize what's really Happening to People.

My Mother also raised me as a Christian, and all seemed to be going well. When I moved into my own Home, the true realities of Life became more apparent, and I often went to Church, for various needs, to Comfort many Ventures daily.

The People, Services, and Music were Great at Church. But I never received what was needed, and after getting Laid Off, from a Temporally Service Job, I briefly stopped attending Church.

Unfortunately, I was Laid Off for Months, but remained undeterred, and applied for Jobs that didn't reply back. So, I found some old Cassette Tapes, from my Mother House, to Record Music off the Radio, during my leisure time, at Home.

After recording 3 songs, "YOU ARE MY LADY, THIS IS HOW WE DO IT, & ONE MORE CHANCE" this, unexpectedly, stopped then reversed to its other side and Played the Matthew Chapter Six.

This was unexpected, I had no idea this was a Bible Audio Cassette. However, it was Narrated Wonderfully, by someone still unknown to me. So, I listened to the whole Chapters available, of the Bible Matthew 1-7, on my audio Cassette.

MICRODECEPTION

Friday, June 7, 1996, I just stopped listening to the Audio Cassette of Matthew. I was walking out the Houses entry, and thought my Landline Phone was off, for non-payment, but this Rung.

Spooky, but I answered the Phone and a Lady asked... "Do you want to work for Chrysler?" I said yes, then she said "Well, we been trying to call you...and can you be here within an hour?"

I said I'll try, and just made it on time to a Job I, ultimately, worked at for eleven years before departing on. But, mysteriously, when I arrived Home from Work, that day, my Phone was off.

I was Bewildered by this...So, I later Contacted the Telephone Company, and no one knew why my Home Phone Worked earlier on that Friday, but it should've been shut-off for non-payment.

At the time, I brushed this off as an error from the Telephone Company. However, I now know this is what Humans call Blessings, and recall others growing up inside Detroit Michigan USA.

All Beings have Purposes, and mostly do things for something. So, I pondered "Why Deities do this for us, and what are we doing for them?" Gods often insist Jobs which Toil Humans, and we rarely know what Evil Things Consumed are made of, and how this Poisons our Bodies daily.

By Darian Vernor Graves

MICRODECEPTION

In the Beginning, I often worked Midnights, for 7 days a week, Making Engines and wanted to Quit my Job for Health reasons. But my Checks were Greater than I ever Earned, and my Rigid Coworkers Courage me to Stay there by saying,

"IT'S A BLESSING TO BE HERE."

My Tribulations there were Epic, but I decided to keep this Job, because much Worse Options were available in Detroit. However, I knew the Hidden Dangers of Working on Assembly Lines.

A year earlier, I worked for a Constructor, that Required us to Paint Industrial Auto Assembly Line Pipes and Black Floors with Lead Paint; this quickly caused Havoc to my Health, and Lead could Stay Embedded in Bones up to 100 Years!

Aliens Conspired Lead to Cause Despondency, and this is a dreadful Illness, that put billions of people on their Knees, Begging God's for Help, since Neolithic times. Lead Toxicity could have your Peers looking like they seen a Ghost, and this Oppression causes the most Suicides today.

Aliens Utilizing Quantum Engineering can live as long as they Desire while Enjoying TUBE. So, they Play Humans for Rapture by Poisoning us, and we Toil for CASH (SEE-ASH). BLESS You is said often. But it's a DROLL (LORD) Word Folks.

By Darian Vernor Graves

MICROECONOMICS.

BLESS =BE-LESS, and Rare Blessings, that chiefly Causes Harm to People, also have Humans Acting like Dogs Waiting to Feed every day. But the GOD'S-PEE-POLES are Bowing daily, and Giving Crueler Beings, in Outer Space, Access to Control Folks Fate.

FUNERAL =FUN-ER-ALL, and Aliens Envy Our Mortality Experiences. So, Humanity really should CATCH-UP (KETCHUP) to Cleverer Alien Micro-economics and know all Dangers of the CON, or DIE-NASTY (DYNASTY).

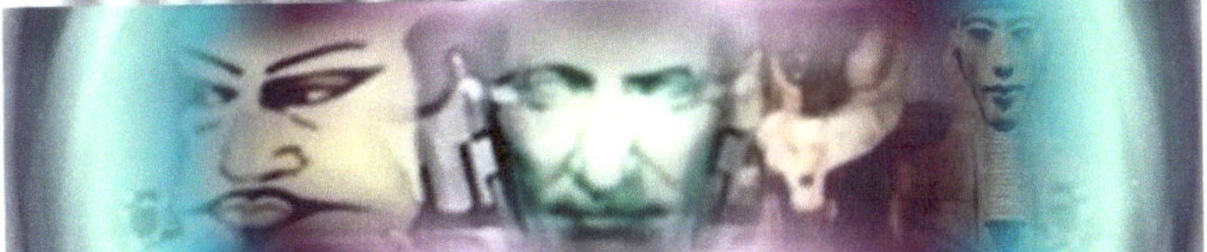

Today, they're over 4,200 Religions and most believe EVIL, which mean LIVE reversed, is also different from their Good God. But they're the same Deities, people Worshiped 5,500 years ago, and change their names likened to Hollywood Mary Pickford's Movie settings.

But Alien God's are staging SERIOUS, which indicates SERIES-US! Moreover, out of all Homophone words, I decoded, DIE-NASTY (DYNASTY) had me pause with aw. Because it started with Lead, Viruses, and Strikes to Humanity Heads, which caused CTE in Catalholyuk.

I later researched People Earliest Civilizations, and all Worshipers described them as Aliens. Sadly, Humans are Complacent from World Leaders, Programmed by the Enemy, who's making ANTS (Insects) out of us.

Kemet God Osiris is, supposedly, from the Spectrum Star SIRIUS (SERIOUS), and Human Ancestors Logged what Aliens insisted them to do for their Sham Peace.

Historically, PEACE has always been a CON, and it's also pronounced as PIECE, because that's truly what it's been, to Humanity, in the last 5,500 years of Strife.

Possibly, Asia first Language risen in Sumeria because the Euphrates River had Monatomic Gold in nimiety. EC Platinum, is also pronounced as Plat, Silver signify Seal, and Gold indicates Goal, because they're steps that made Folks 24-Hour Live Conductors for Display.

Gold was also called, "THE FLESH OF GODS" and it Circulates through Folks Bloodstream like Flowing Nanowires; this cleverly enhance Visions, Sounds, and Smells in our Pineal Gland (3RD EYE) like a TV.

Aliens Channeled Languages in Scribes and Priest; they utilized Gold to make Vivid Visions, Sounds, and Smells of our Families to Market the Afterlife.

Aliens also Program Humans, like Software, when Praying to God's. Furthermore, to Control People Fate, they need Humankind to Worship them, just like Updating Software, to Stage Mischief for Fun.

What pleasures do Aliens receive from Humanity? Well, 1000s in every desire people often Quest for in Entertainment, Love, and Adventures on Earth, that are also Stored likened to a Video Game App.

CHARM =SEE-HARM, and Creating Vivid Simulated People are the most Toiling things, Human Beings can do, in Digital Entertainment. So, Actors Wear Simulation Suits, to Produce this Hard Work today.

Eureka, because Realism is Key, Producing Perfect Simulated Beings are Toiling, and folks live on an Extraordinary Planet with Authentic Scenery daily.

As a result, it's easier to CON Humans, fool people to Toil for Making Live Entertainment Raptures, & Downloading Humanity Souls likened to Software.

Persistence

BE-TRAY (BETRAY), & BORDER =BE-ORDER like a Cruel Menu, but no-one should Fear another Human. Sadly, World Leaders are Proficient Butchers, to People that Betray, for Maintaining the PEE-OW-ER (POWER).

After Poisoning Humans Health with Lead, which caused Hardship and put Prayers on their Knees often. MORE-KNEE (MONEY) also does this too, and it's Alien God's Bait.

Alien Money Hustles have People on their Knees, Praying for Jobs, that also Toil them until their Broken, in Wild Competition for Business, Entertainment, Factories, Sports, and folks should never do this at any Price.

PRICE =PEE-OUR-ICE. The Earth's Covered with more EC Metals than ever now; from Transports, Factories, and Home Dwellings Filled with Copper, for Alien's Amusement.

This Pitiful PLAY-NETWORK is Flourishing, and the DOG Controls Human Beings Fate. So, I Created this Book for Humankind to, "INSIGHT TO WHAT'S RIGHT" and let's Try to BE-RIGHT-ESTABLISHED (BRIGHTEST)... A Simple way, to Achieve this, are Learning Homophone Words to Dim Alien Programs.

Persistence

CRIMINAL =SEE-RIM-IN-ALL

HUMAN BEING =WHO-MAN-BEING

ACT-KNOW-LEDGE (ACKNOWLEDGE)

A =A, B =BE, C =SEE, D =DE, LL =L N =IN

Words that begin with the letters above and ends with a full word are often what it also signifies. Example: ALIEN =A-LIEN, BEER (ALCOHOL) =BE-ER, & ICON =I-CON.

Palindrome words or numbers like EVE and 313 are only pronounced as shown. Anadrome words like MAD =DAM, EVIL =LIVE, and WALL =LAW can be reversed.

Full words are often split up in shorter comical meanings. Example: GRIDLOCK =GRID AND OUR MISFORTUNE =FORTUNE.

Homophone are the roots of most words pronounced the same and are comedic meanings. Example: ADULT =A-DOLT, BAD =BE-ADVERTISEMENT, BETRAYAL =BETRAY-ALL, BEAT =BE-AT, BLAST =BE-LAST, BLOW =BE-LOW, BOX =BE-OXEN, BRAVE =BE-RAVE, CLOWN =SEE-LOW-INSIDE, MANAGER =MAN-AGER, PAID =PEE-AID, PEOPLE =PEE-POLE, PLOT =PEE-LOT, & PRIDE =PEE-RIDE.

The 1st 1-5 letters are often the meaning of fullest word pronounced before suffix. Example: CASTLE =CAST, PLAN =PLAY-INSIDE, PLEASE =PLEA, & TRUST =TRUE.

The First Widely Utilized Language appeared in Africa called Medu Neter (Word of God), it can also be seen on Clay Tablets around 5500 years ago. However, it's been logged that this came from Extraterrestrial God's.

CREW =SEE-OUR-EW. Languages, which number over 7000 & growing now, also divided Human Beings with Prejudice. Alien God's Religion and Languages Created numerous Diabolical Cultures, for Cruel Entertainment.

Ta-Seti & Kemet's Medu Neter Language Symbols are easier for folks to Learn, with Words like AUSET which means AU-SET; this also seems to be deprived because AU symbol is cleverly Gold and Astronomical Unit now.

Medu Neter is Blacklisted because it's too easy for the masses to Learn and can Unify Human Beings. So, the BE-LACK-HEADS (BLACKHEADS) Educated Sumerians a harder second Language which led to 1000s, to keep people divided, and AUSET was renamed to Greek ISIS.

Kemet also means "Black Land." But the word BLACK signify BE-LACK, and this is what this Desert Country saw for over 3,000 years of Strife. No-one is the Color BLACK or WHITE which isn't RIGHT folks, because we need the Suns Vitamin D; I'll explain Kemet more later.

PEOPLE =PEE-POLE to Humiliate Human Existence for Entertainment; God's excel by enhancing inhibitors & DOPAMINE (DOPE-A-MEN) for folks to act Buffoonery.

LAW =WALL reversed, and Humankind is often being Programmed, by Depraved Divinities, to Insight Inside the WALL. So, People only see what's inside the BOX (BE-OXEN) and this, cleverly, Limits their Intellect now.

The Lightest and Darkest Skin Humans risen less than 7,000 years ago, by Family Incest, that Created more. Multiple Languages also Divided Humanity more than Skin Color does and Continues to Cause Ridicule daily.

SMARTER =SMART-ER, and Prejudice Programs made more Humanity Races, like Breeds of Dogs, in the last 7,000 years. So, oppressing other Ethnics, for Financial Gains on Earth, is making Humanity Smart Weapons, Against Ourselves, and prolong God's PLAY-NETWORK.

Global Warming is Rising from Super Pollution, led by Broken Engine Transports being dumped near Africa's Equator, with missing Catalytic Converters, Producing Smoke. Are they Aimed to Lower African Populations?

KNOWLEDGE =KNOW-LEDGE. So, be Aware of all the Words meaning we Speak and the CON of Civilization. LEDGE is also defined as, "A narrow horizontal surface projecting from a wall or cliff" and this exposes Alien God's Agenda. So, INSIGHT TO WHAT'S RIGHT, think outside this WALL, and Defeat GOD DAM (MAD DOG).

CROWN =SEE-OUR-OWN, like 360-Degree Cameras & Ancient Kohl Black Cosmetics, worn around Eyes, that Contains Lead does the same. But Lead would've also Poisoned Folks Health from Bremsstrahlung Radiation.

COMA =SEE-OMA, by the God's CON. Those who were called Nomadic was self-sufficient, and often Free of Sham Religions, that produced Alien's PLAY-NETWORK.

CRISIS =SEE-OUR-IS-IS, and they are not Playing Folks! So, avoid being MORE-ON (MORON) to Religions aw, which caused all Slavery, Wars, and Murders for Shows.

CONDOM =SEE-ON-DUMB, and this is a Sex Warning! Nomadic Folk, Living in Africa, were also Childbearing at much Older Ages, which Human DNA confirm today.

MASTURBATE =MASTER-BAIT, and the PEE-LAY (PLAY) also do this by Depriving Lifespans from Diseases and Diminished Essential Minerals often. So, Alien's likely only have Simulated Sex, for sustaining their Longevity.

DOCTORED =DOCTOR. Mainstream Toiling Jobs are a Deceit for Pleasure; including Humans Suffering from Illnesses that, frequently, goes to these, supposedly, Qualified Health Physicians called Doctors, which are Educated to DOCK Human Beings Fitness with 100s of PRE-SCRIPTS (PRESCRIPTION) for Harsh Entertainment.

DOCTORED Agendas like inserting Gadolinium Heavy Metals, inside our Veins, are a CON for Sinister Aliens Butchering Amusement every day. So, 1000s are being Misled to do, unnecessary, gloomy Surgeries each year.

Humankind can live unthinkable Ages, but Extraterrestrials are folks real MAN-AGER! Cut, what was that...are you kidding me? Drink this WHISKEY (RISKY). Play the Role! Hit him with the Pitch! Take a Drug, make them Laugh. Loose a Finger and Win that SHAM-PEE-ON-SHIP (CHAMPIONSHIP). So, insight toward living Leisurely, Healthy, and Protect your only Body from MAN-AGER'S (MANAGERS) by avoiding them daily folks.

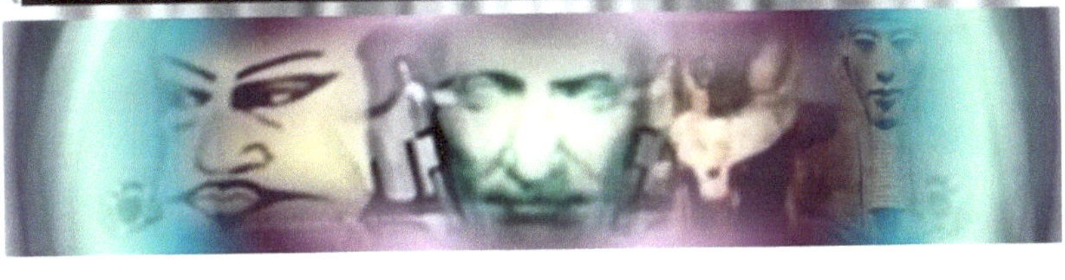

WARRANT =WAR-OUR-ANT

DENTIST =DENT. A-MALL-GUM (AMALGAM) Tooth Fillings are an example of how distain we've become as a Species, Programmed by Microdeception, today.

When folks combine EC Metals together, the more it Leaches in the Air. But Amalgam's TAKES THE CAKE, because it is also a Battery inside Humanities Mouth!

Foul Dentist put Toxic Mercury, Silver, and Copper in Amalgam Tooth Fillings, that Leaches like Cigarette Smoke, under Ultraviolet Light. Sadly, we will never Truly be Beings, until Humanity Abolish Profits made from Chronic Health, which are causing Birth Defects.

POLICEMEN: PO is defined shorter for POOR, and all this signifies POOR-LICE-MEN. So, try seeking a Job which doesn't CON, and the title should be your Fate.

Furthermore, this Copper Badge also has Policemen Programmed MORE-ON (MORON). But if you follow these Courts Money, you'll find the Bigger Criminals.

Authorities Profit off Crime, Corruption, and run the Biggest Gang (Police) in each US City. But the Enemy is also fond of Humanity Prisons, Police Beat Downs, and numerous Injustice from Live Court Experiences.

Nevertheless, PO-LICE-MEN takes the Devils Bait and have Immunity to hold people for False Charges, Bail Ransom, then also Kill without regard of Human Life **DURING THEIR WAR-RANTS CALLED "WARRANT."**

JUSTICE (JUST-ICE), and PROBATE =PRO-BAIT. This is precisely what Humans will receive, in this recurring Court System, that's becoming more Corrupt yearly.

It amazes me how Government Constitutions could CON Folks and pretend to stop Crime, when they're mostly profiting a third of their Economies from this.

Most USA People, Accused of a Crime, are Innocent & often saw A-TURN-KNEE (ATTORNEY) in Courts. This is Conspired from Police, Attorney's, Clerks, and Judges Working Underhanded for SEE-ASH (CASH). So, Video Evidence is also despised, and thwart now.

MICROECONOMICS.

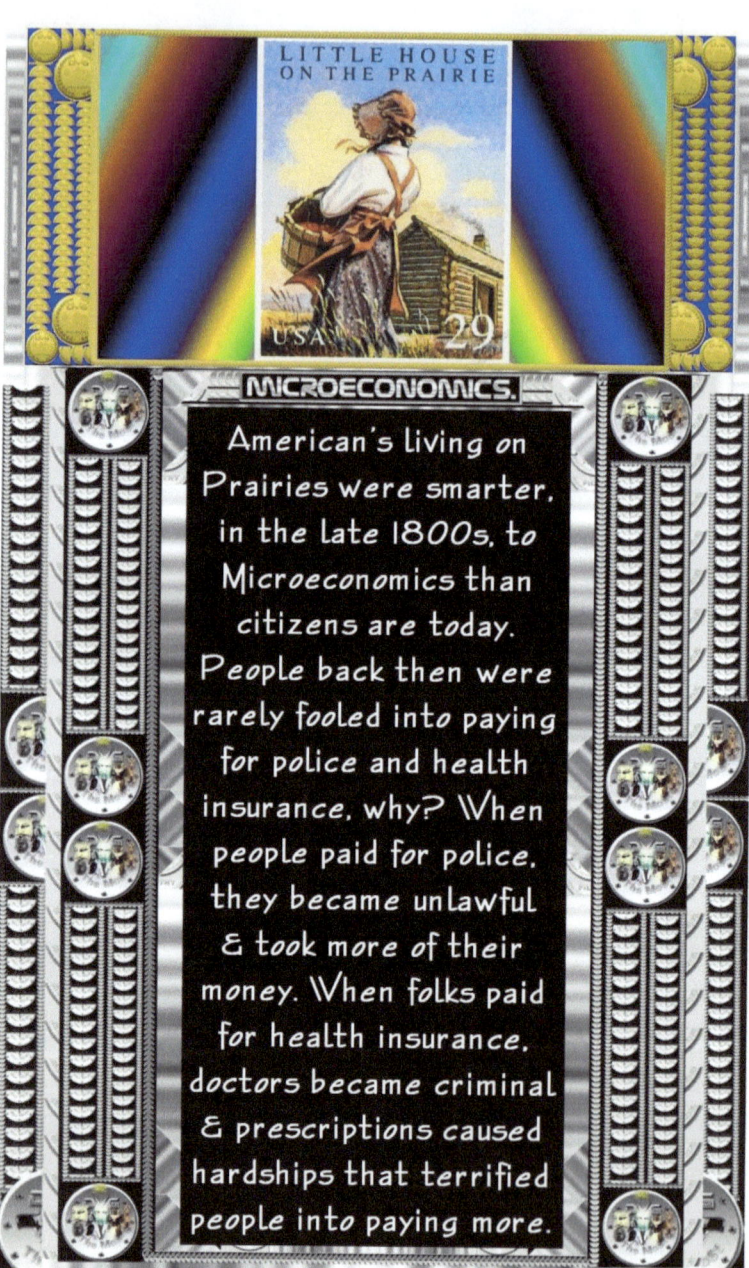

American's living on Prairies were smarter, in the late 1800s, to Microeconomics than citizens are today. People back then were rarely fooled into paying for police and health insurance, why? When people paid for police, they became unlawful & took more of their money. When folks paid for health insurance, doctors became criminal & prescriptions caused hardships that terrified people into paying more.

BEST =BE-ESTABLISHED, and Micro-deception persists by CON. People are also Bribed by Money do this. So, utilizing Video Recordings, to Protect Ourselves from Injustice, are often being hindered inside Courthouses for the District A-TURN-KNEE (ATTORNEY) Profits too.

BE-TRAY-ALL (BETRAYAL) is LAW by WALL. But many Students Insight being like the Attorney Perry Mason, who Defends Falsely Accused Folks on TV Courtroom Drama. Amusing, but very far from how these Alien Scripts of CON Entertainment Works daily Youngsters.

CASTLE =CAST. Castles had it all occur under one roof like Murder, Rape, Courts, and Jails. So, beware of this MAD DOG (GOD DAM) and DEVIL, who has LIVED the TUBE Life from Stealing Human Beings Soul every day.

Now turn your TV Programs Audio on Mute; this can, temporarily, uncover this MEN-ACE (MENACE) Affairs. After this is achieved, you could see what I do. People are a Comedic Show and Alien's are making Bonnie & Clyde out of our Lives, like Cars Crash Dummies, daily.

Today, Human Beings are in dire straits, and is served a BE-LO-VIDEO (BELOVED). Moreover, People's Display Begins Live, when the I-CON (ICON) wakes up inside their Bedroom, Prison Cell, or Battlefield yarning now.

Aliens choose to Script our Dues, with Epic Rules. So, don't be discouraged from MISS-TAKES (MISTAKES) in Life, because they're Staging Scenes for a better Show.

ALTAR =ALTER.

BITCH =BE-ITCH, and we're being divided by GAY-ME (GAME) Programs. So, there's a Gay Stigma on Bright Rainbow Colors now to deter most people not utilize them. However, these Excel our Intellect and Aliens are Enraptured by Human Beings Naïve Actions daily.

Marriage Vows started about 4800 years ago, inside Kemet, with Gold Wedding Bands that Staged Strife, Altered Human Lives, and the CHEAP still SEE-HEAP.

HUSBAND =WHO'S-BAND? And those who Marry at Altars Lives will be Altered like Comical Sitcoms. Deir el-Medina Ostraca Stones reveal how we lived 3,300 years ago and CHEAT =SEE-HEAT! Unruly Demeanor with others and Tribulations were the same as today.

In-fact, they talked about similar Taxes, Style, Sexual Desires, and Threatening Murder Plots aimed at folks Sleeping with People Beloved Partner or Spouse were common in Ancient Times. Nevertheless, this is the PEE-ART-INSIDE-ER (PARTNER), which are Alien God Scripted Recurring Programs, for Live Entertainment.

ALTER is shorter for Alternator, and has Worshipers, unknowingly, walking counterclockwise around Alien BOX (BE-OXEN) of Dark Forces, since Ancient Kemet Times. So, the ALTAR (ALTER) is Programming Folks Pathological and utilized like a Demolition Machine. Sadly, it's still causing Strife, Murder, & World Crisis.

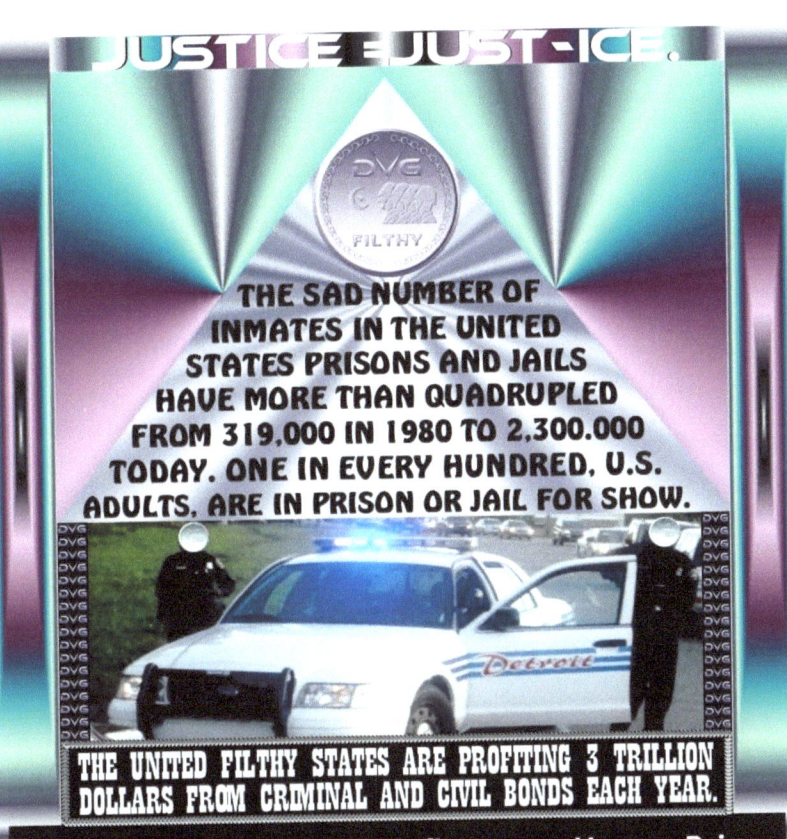

JUSTICE =JUST-ICE.

THE SAD NUMBER OF INMATES IN THE UNITED STATES PRISONS AND JAILS HAVE MORE THAN QUADRUPLED FROM 319,000 IN 1980 TO 2,300.000 TODAY. ONE IN EVERY HUNDRED, U.S. ADULTS, ARE IN PRISON OR JAIL FOR SHOW.

THE UNITED FILTHY STATES ARE PROFITING 3 TRILLION DOLLARS FROM CRIMINAL AND CIVIL BONDS EACH YEAR.

ANTHEM =ANT-HIM. This influence us Human Beings to Toil Entertainers, Athletes, Armies, and frequently, CON like Dirty Politicians, for Showcasing Amusement.

The Microeconomics of LAW by WALL is at its pinnacle of CON, in The United States of America for Profit, and this Underhandedness with Buddies are Pathetic today.

Sadly, we are still taking the Devils Bait termed CASH and this is Prolonging Cruelty to others for Alien God's Rapture. So, this must be Abolished for our Persistence.

-ABRAHAM LINCOLN

Today, Politician's creating CON Laws, to make more Cash Money, are now Pathological without Senses, for people, to do the right things. Sadly, their Greed are making millions of good Families Fail yearly; this is causing a Wave of more Crime, Poverty, and Chaos in Humankind's future today.

The Giant USA Criminals are Lawyers, Police, and Judges Scheming Underhandedness to SEE-ASH (CASH). So, Clients and Jurors should say No to Court Cases that's now an expanding Enterprise, by also putting Innocent people in Prison, today.

This JUST-ICE (JUSTICE) Network is 100 percent CON for Profit, and not a Tenth of a Penny less. So, The African Truth recommends that Humans Record Suspicious Encounters and avoid Courts, or also Practice being a Pro-Se Litigant if needed.

Courts and Prisons are Devil Displays for Rapture and no-one should be put behind Bars with this Mischief. Victims are also released from Jail with a Criminal Record, to deprive them from getting a good Job, and this prolong Human Oppression.

MISLEAD =MISS-LEAD

BRIGHTMOOR WAR MEMORIAL inspired me to write this Book, and it means BE-RIGHT-MORE. So, the most important Topic, I'd like to Insight for Humanity, are the Dangers to People Health.

Historically, LEAD (Atomic #82) was utilized as a Hardship Element, to keep People Unhealthy. LEAD-ER (LEADER) is also the first Heavy Metal Humans Smelted, and this was being Produced inside Catalhoyuk City, around 8500 years ago.

The Younger Dryas lasted for 1000 years, and, possibly, Campfires had Lead inside Stones. But we didn't Smelt this Metal in our 200,000 year History. So, Higher Levels of EC Platinum, from a Comet Explosion...enhanced Alien God's Hold.

SPIRIT =SPEAR-IT, and LEAD oldest known usage are Beads People were duped to put over their Heads, for ridding Spirits, during Neolithic Times.

This was mostly influenced to Poison Humanity Health. Spiritual Rituals that often uses Chakra Stones and Sage Burning also cause Harm to us.

Lead Deprived the Sumerians, Kemetians, and Romans Health; it was often used as Kohl Black Makeup, around our Eyes, in Kemet and Sumer.

Rome was also Insisted to use Pure Lead Water Pipes, and duped to put this Metal inside Wine! This Poisoned Millions for Alien God's Raptures.

By Darian Vernor Graves

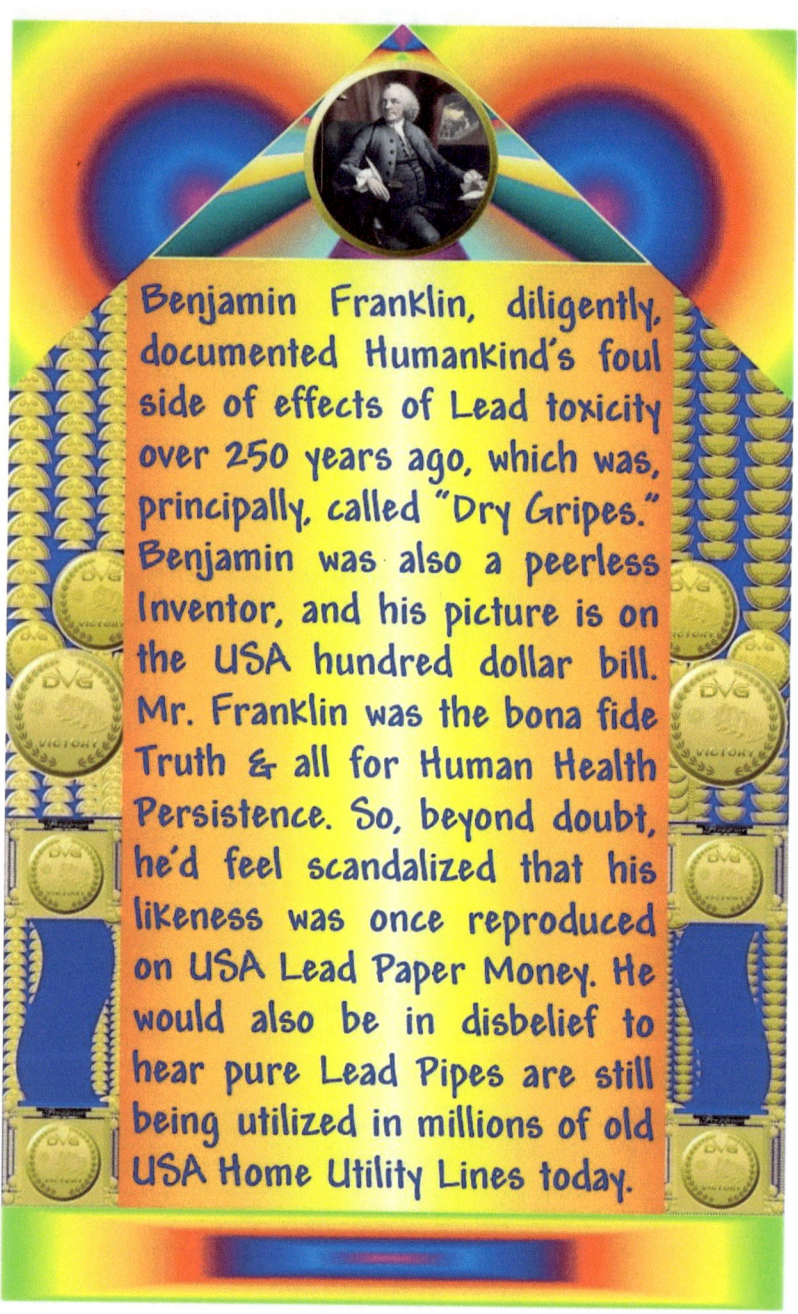

Benjamin Franklin, diligently, documented Humankind's foul side of effects of Lead toxicity over 250 years ago, which was, principally, called "Dry Gripes." Benjamin was also a peerless Inventor, and his picture is on the USA hundred dollar bill. Mr. Franklin was the bona fide Truth & all for Human Health Persistence. So, beyond doubt, he'd feel scandalized that his likeness was once reproduced on USA Lead Paper Money. He would also be in disbelief to hear pure Lead Pipes are still being utilized in millions of old USA Home Utility Lines today.

MISLEAD =MISS-LEAD

Today, Humankind World LEAD-ER'S (LEADERS) are Programmed to BE-ILL (BILL), and can't stop Water Pipes being Soldiered with Lead; this also Leach inside Homes and Sewers by Roof Shingles.

HIGH-ER (HIGHER) Lead can cause Inflammation from Head to Toe and is Relentless. Sadly, people could see these Mainstream Doctors for Decades and seldom be told they have Lead Toxicity, why?

Lead could stay embedded in Human Bodies for 100 years! Children are, primary, Diagnosed with Lead Toxicity, because their Growing Bones and Organs are pushing it back into the Bloodstream.

Dense Lead Superior Jolts are like Battery Coils in Bones, and increases the Watts, in our Bodies, that have many layers like floors on a Skyscraper.

Lead doesn't subside easily and increases, like an Hourglass, inside Humanity Bones overtime. But Levels can Fluctuate, and Collapse likened to the awful NYC Twin Towers destruction, forming -Itis.

Thomas Midgley Jr. was MISS-LEAD from WHIZ-DUMB (WISDOM) to produce Tetraethyl Lead, in Bad Gasoline Engine Transports, during the 1920s.

The Lead Transports Poisoned Billions of Human Beings and it still Affects our Environment today. Sadly, we continue to use Lead for God's Rapture.

By Darian Vernor Graves

Human's oldest known medical procedure was the Enema and it, supposedly, came from the Kemetic God Thoth, for detoxing. Enemas can give us decent results, but pots and containers often leached EC Metals or Chemicals in liquids.

Extraterrestrials utilized Copper for leaching in Pots and Enema Containers to increase their reception in users. As a youngster, I recall not preferring to cook my eggs on cast Iron skillets, because it also leached and turned them black.

Today, our Health Procedures still come from Alien's and folk take their luxury bait to persist this CON. So, avoid bad goods, utilize Smart Water & Air Detectors to maintain your Health.

-ABRAHAM LINCOLN

How do these politicians smile &, habitually, shake each other filthier hands knowing this health CON is breeding more children born with Autism today? I suspect drinking alcohol along with snorting their cocaine through a buffet of the devils bribed bait cash are programming these dim fiends what to articulate. CASH =SEE-ASH & they no-longer have a backbone to upgrade their health for persistence now; let alone

HUMANITY?

POSSESSION

Extraterrestrial Gods are likely Possessing multiple Beings, on Earthly Planets, by also utilizing Comet Blast; these objects contain Gateway EC Elements like Platinum/Aluminum, and also Compounds like Carbon Dioxide/Ammonia to Oppress their Health.

Possession Compounds are still utilized for Farms, Factories, Bleach (Ammonia) and Transports make Platinum/Aluminum Catalytic Converter Emissions. Sadly, it seems nobody is realizing this CON today?

Humankind is often Oppressed by Microdeception Programs which also have a WALL (LAW), that can make folks Sick, or have Bad Luck, whenever they get out of line, to persists this CON Entertainment.

Extraterrestrial Gods are remorseless! They utilized Toxic Lead Consumption to mislead Humanity who thought they had Good Intentions for them. But it caused Despondency, put folks on their Knees, and people still beg these Flagrant Gods for help today.

After Humankind Hardship, from Lead Poison, was achieved from the Masses; clever Alien God's later marketed numerous misleading Religions, Temples, and Immortality, that, sadly, still thrives every day.

Hardship from Lead Toxicity, likely, also influenced Farming Crops for Alcohol, and this, Momentarily, made people feel better during the Neolithic Ages.

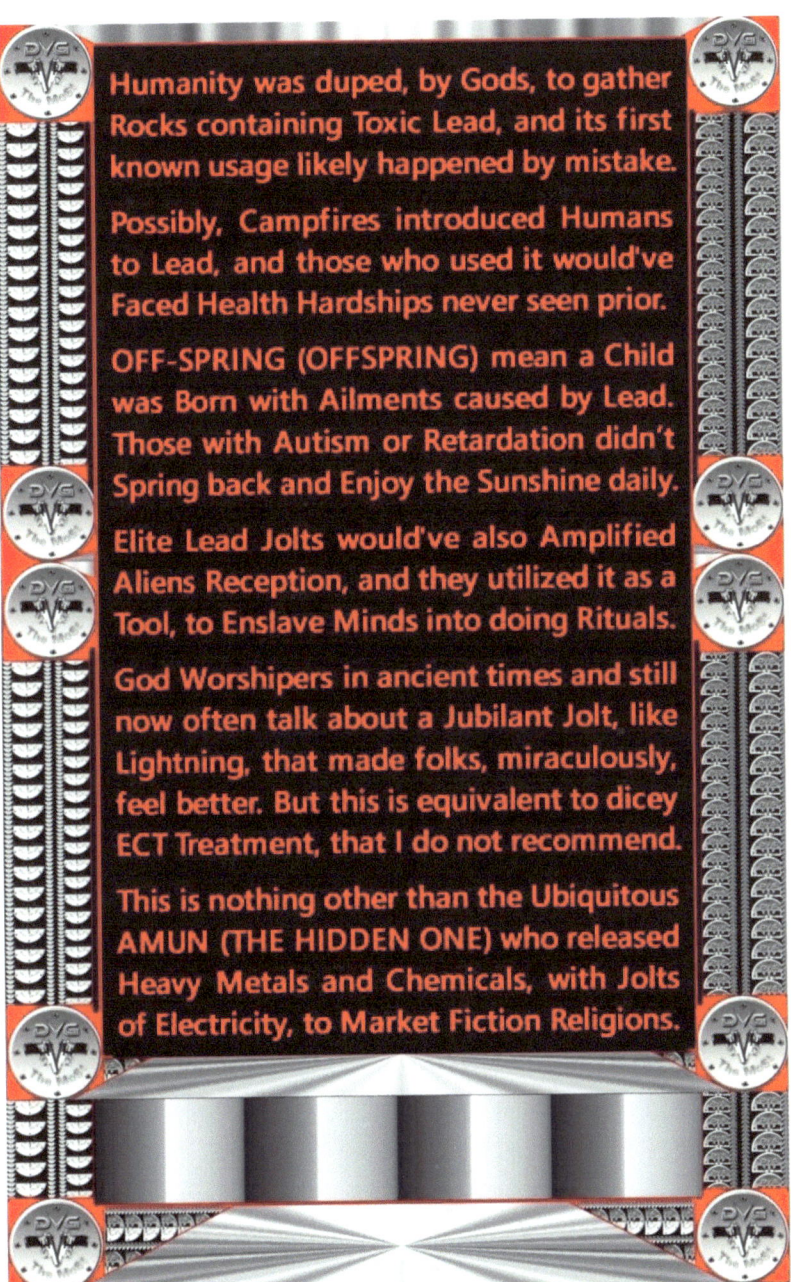

Humanity was duped, by Gods, to gather Rocks containing Toxic Lead, and its first known usage likely happened by mistake.

Possibly, Campfires introduced Humans to Lead, and those who used it would've Faced Health Hardships never seen prior.

OFF-SPRING (OFFSPRING) mean a Child was Born with Ailments caused by Lead. Those with Autism or Retardation didn't Spring back and Enjoy the Sunshine daily.

Elite Lead Jolts would've also Amplified Aliens Reception, and they utilized it as a Tool, to Enslave Minds into doing Rituals.

God Worshipers in ancient times and still now often talk about a Jubilant Jolt, like Lightning, that made folks, miraculously, feel better. But this is equivalent to dicey ECT Treatment, that I do not recommend.

This is nothing other than the Ubiquitous AMUN (THE HIDDEN ONE) who released Heavy Metals and Chemicals, with Jolts of Electricity, to Market Fiction Religions.

Losing Weight doesn't remove Heavy Metals. Try Stretch Exercising, Nutrition Protocols, & rid them by the Sun.

Today, natural Zeolite works Superior to Extract Heavy Metals by Bonding to them, like Magnets, and removes them. But it can also take years, to take Toxins out properly, without causing Harm.

Ancient Kemetic people stepped on Nile Catfish, which packs 400 Volts, to Jolt Despondency out their System; I don't recommend this, because it can also damage Nerves or stop the Heart today.

Prevention is Key, because it's harder to remove Heavy Metals. However, for severe cases, limited device Jolts weekly, to folks Feet, should reduce Despondency without causing damage overtime.

Limited Jolts perform like Electrolysis, which can release Channels of Heavy Elements, Chemicals, and Viruses embedded deeper inside our Bones.

Pneumonia is often deadly because of Immune response overreactions to Heavy EC Elements causing fibrosis in the lungs. Cigarette Tobacco smoke leaches Polonium-210 (Atomic #84) and just one pack could be over a 100 times more Radioactive than a X-RAY. So, Cancer is certain!

Today, the average Human Eat and Drink less than ten pounds daily, but most perceive that's more than the air they breathe in a day. But, a person also takes around 20,000 breaths and consume 35 pounds of air daily. So, controlling what people breathe is a #1 priority for Health.

Mainstream Homes are loaded with nasty pure Heavy Elements, Chemicals, and Mold which Poison our bodies. So, we can, easily, produce houses, cookware, and hygiene products made out of natural items; doing this and breathing clean air can boost our average lifespan 50%.

Humanities largest organ, which is the skin, is also absorbing pounds each year. So, keeping this clear of Demolishing Chemicals and Heavy Elements will extend people's life expectancy.

As a youngster, I would often enjoy watching Sun Rays shine on Dust through my window at home; I also researched and learned that up to ninety-nine percent of Dusts, in Homes, come from Humans who live in them or Pets today.

Dust is a Waste, it's Loaded with Unessential Elements, that are harmful to Human Bodies, and Cleaning daily is essential to remove this.

Humankind also shouldn't use Carpets, Paint with Chemicals, Bedding which stores Dust, Mercury Light Bulbs, Cookware that Leaches Metals, and folks must keep their Air Clear, with Central Filtration, for Optimum Health.

Today, what we Eat and Drink will determine how many years folks are going to Live Well. Nevertheless, most believe, "an Apple a day keeps the Doctors away." But I say, an Apple a day will take your Health Persistence away.

Perilous Apples are full of Organ Degrading Fructose, and Seeds with Poisonous Arsenic! Although, Fructose is an Essential Enzyme & our Body produce this. So, it should rarely be consumed inside Foods and never pure form.

In the Body, High Levels of Fructose is like a Grinder on Metal. But most folks often think Sugar (Fructose) only rotten their Teeth daily.

But it also Demolition Bones, Organs, Blood, and Nerves. Sadly, the average USA person, Consumes over 100 Pounds of Sugar yearly!

MICRODECEPTION

CANDY =SEE-A-INSIDE-DIE. Alien's marketed fiddled histories like A-DAM (ADAM) and EVE which deceived people to eat Apples or Sugar rich foods, like CAKE (SEE-ACHE) at Weddings, for reducing Human Beings lifespan every day.

Alien Gods Obesity fattened us up for pleasure by marketing Venus Figurines and taught folks how to butcher wild animals and themselves!

Extraterrestrials also influenced people to Farm and consume perilous Grains, with Chemicals, which decreased the IQ of our Brains for show.

All the 92 Elements are unsafe to Humankind bodies in pure form and our Possessions which degrade, in people homes, increase this effect.

Electro-conductivity Elements like Copper and Aluminum are baited to leach inside kitchens; this increase Extraterrestrials Live Reception in people each time they cook meals for Display.

Historically, Cookware has degraded Humans Health daily, from raw Elements, and this also continues to ravage Humankind bodies today.

Beware! This mild burnt taste, from Cookware foods, are coming from the enormous amount of Iron, Steel, Aluminum, or Copper leaching in it; this includes perilous Glass Cookware and Cups that are mostly made of toxic Lead today.

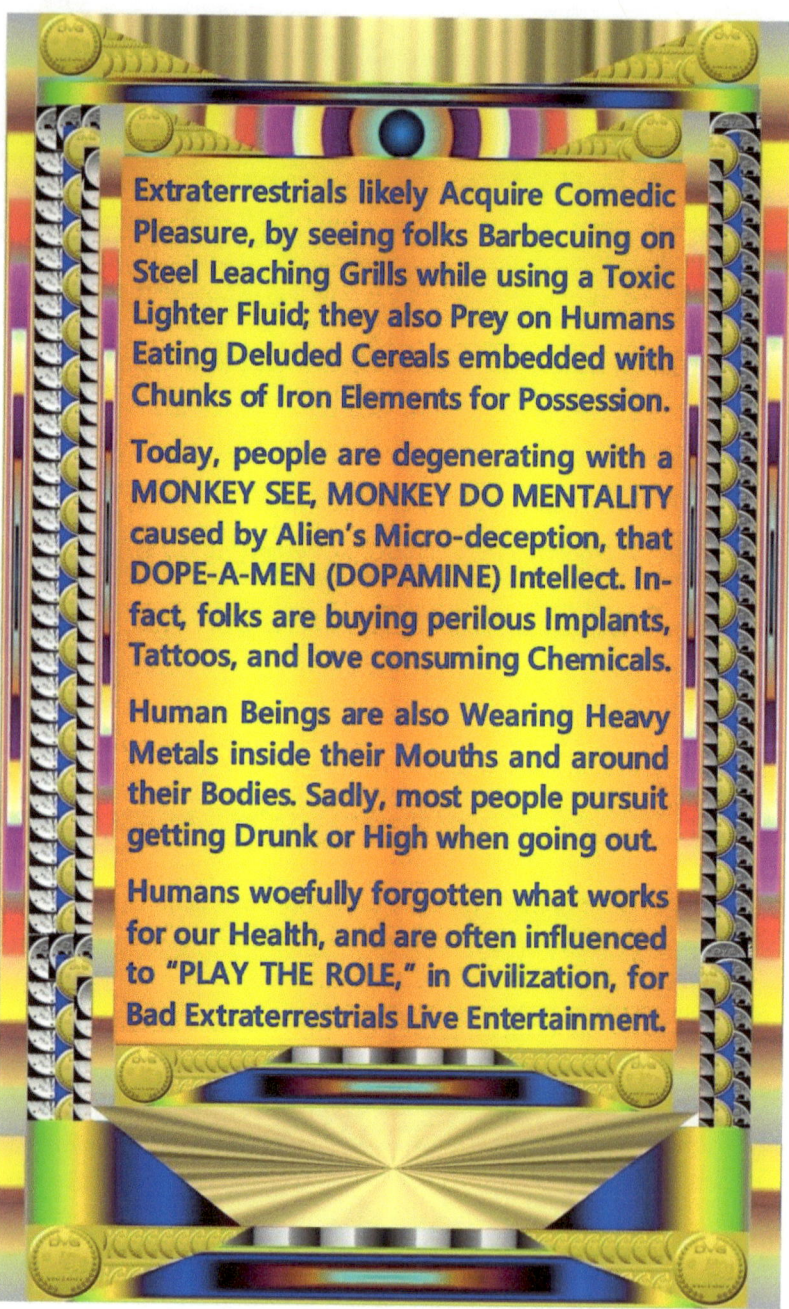

Extraterrestrials likely Acquire Comedic Pleasure, by seeing folks Barbecuing on Steel Leaching Grills while using a Toxic Lighter Fluid; they also Prey on Humans Eating Deluded Cereals embedded with Chunks of Iron Elements for Possession.

Today, people are degenerating with a MONKEY SEE, MONKEY DO MENTALITY caused by Alien's Micro-deception, that DOPE-A-MEN (DOPAMINE) Intellect. In-fact, folks are buying perilous Implants, Tattoos, and love consuming Chemicals.

Human Beings are also Wearing Heavy Metals inside their Mouths and around their Bodies. Sadly, most people pursuit getting Drunk or High when going out.

Humans woefully forgotten what works for our Health, and are often influenced to "PLAY THE ROLE," in Civilization, for Bad Extraterrestrials Live Entertainment.

Disease = Dis-ease

Today, Humankind believes wearing Gold, Copper, and Silver Jewelry are harmless? Although, they're also Batteries which will cause Eternal Pain today.

All Table Elements contain Energy, and our Bodies are also weaker Electromagnets. So, people being Exposed to Larger Quantities, of these Heavier EC Elements from Cookware and Paints, will increase the Watts throughout Humans Whole Body, how?

Grasp an Iron Clothing Hanger and nudge it with a Stronger Battery, this should make it a powerful Electromagnet. Heavy Metals have more Gauss & Pulls Harder as they Accumulate inside our Bones; Stacking more Magnets, over a Refrigerator, could Demonstrate how unyielding these are to remove.

When High Electromagnetism circulates in people Bones and Veins, it will do the same. But Doctors Profit from -ITIS, and this is a DIS-EASE (DISEASE).

Heavy Metals coalesce in folks Cardiovascular and Central Nervous System; causing many Organs to fail. This is the Enemy long recurring Sinister Plan, for Display, and it's called DIE-NASTY (DYNASTY)!

Why haven't we solved these simple Oppressions? Well, it's the DEMOLITION-INSIDE (DEMON) us all, and Humans are Pathological by PLAY-NETWORK Wealth; this also Hinder Insight with CON Schools.

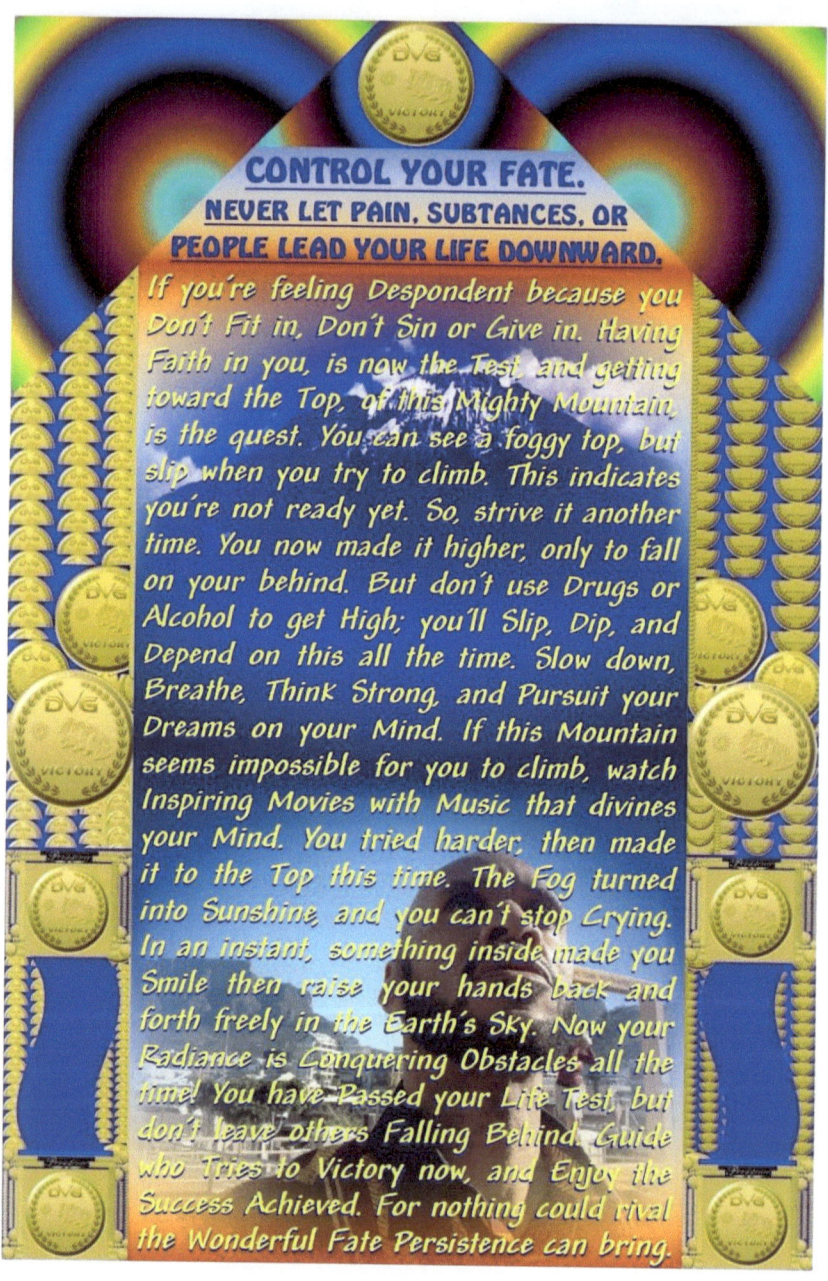

CONTROL YOUR FATE.

NEVER LET PAIN, SUBTANCES, OR PEOPLE LEAD YOUR LIFE DOWNWARD.

If you're feeling Despondent because you Don't Fit in, Don't Sin or Give in. Having Faith in you, is now the Test, and getting toward the Top, of this Mighty Mountain, is the quest. You can see a foggy top, but slip when you try to climb. This indicates you're not ready yet. So, strive it another time. You now made it higher, only to fall on your behind. But don't use Drugs or Alcohol to get High; you'll Slip, Dip, and Depend on this all the time. Slow down, Breathe, Think Strong, and Pursuit your Dreams on your Mind. If this Mountain seems impossible for you to climb, watch Inspiring Movies with Music that divines your Mind. You tried harder, then made it to the Top this time. The Fog turned into Sunshine, and you can't stop Crying. In an instant, something inside made you Smile then raise your hands back and forth freely in the Earth's Sky. Now your Radiance is Conquering Obstacles all the time! You have Passed your Life Test, but don't leave others Falling Behind. Guide who Tries to Victory now, and Enjoy the Success Achieved. For nothing could rival the Wonderful Fate Persistence can bring.

AKHENATEN & QUEEN NEFERTITI ABOLISHED ALL THE GOD'S AND WORSHIPED THE ATEN (SUN).

Akhenaten & Nefertiti

On December 25th, Jesus Birthday is celebrated and billions of Human Beings, around this World now, are thanking him for the Faith it brings to their Lives. But over a dozen similar God's like Krishna, Osiris, Horus, and Tammuz are also celebrated this same day today.

This was chiefly because THE WINTER SOLSTICE and ZODIAC CYCLE mesmerized Ancient Human Beings, who thought Stars were these Alien God's, they seen glowing in Orbs (THE HIDDEN ONE), that people still document Globally today. Unquestionably, Humanity was double-crossed by God's which, horribly, persists.

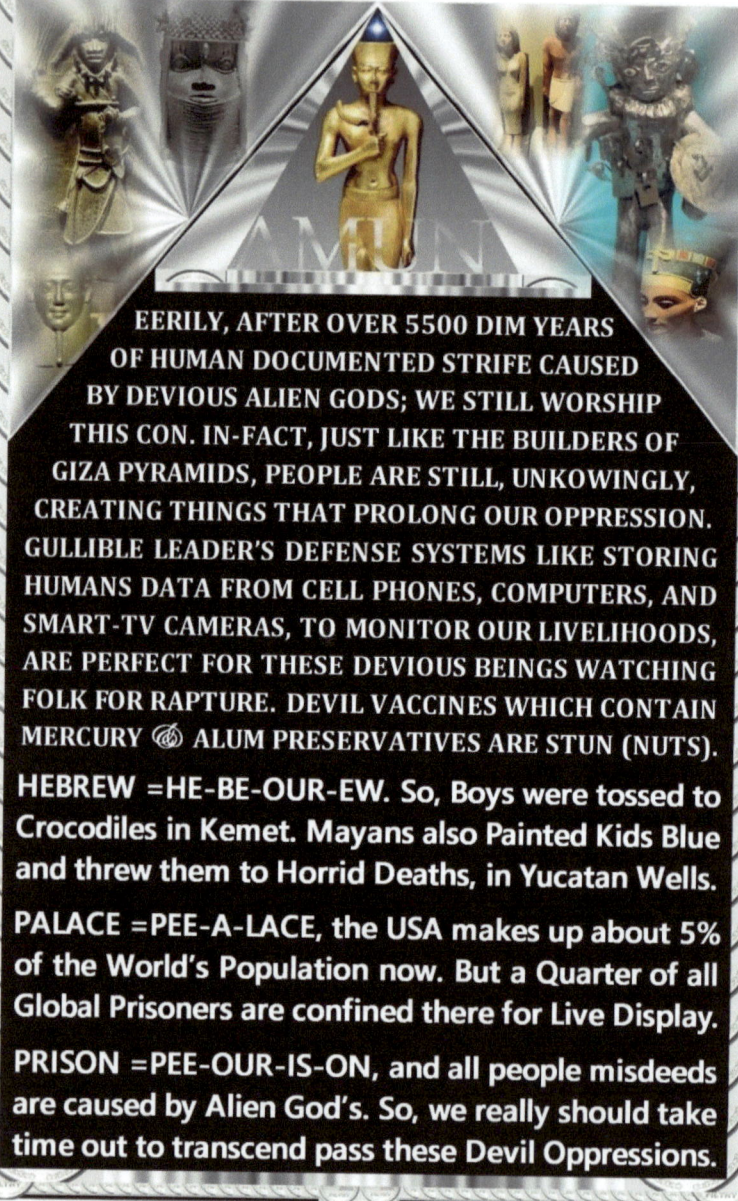

EERILY, AFTER OVER 5500 DIM YEARS OF HUMAN DOCUMENTED STRIFE CAUSED BY DEVIOUS ALIEN GODS; WE STILL WORSHIP THIS CON. IN-FACT, JUST LIKE THE BUILDERS OF GIZA PYRAMIDS, PEOPLE ARE STILL, UNKOWINGLY, CREATING THINGS THAT PROLONG OUR OPPRESSION. GULLIBLE LEADER'S DEFENSE SYSTEMS LIKE STORING HUMANS DATA FROM CELL PHONES, COMPUTERS, AND SMART-TV CAMERAS, TO MONITOR OUR LIVELIHOODS, ARE PERFECT FOR THESE DEVIOUS BEINGS WATCHING FOLK FOR RAPTURE. DEVIL VACCINES WHICH CONTAIN MERCURY & ALUM PRESERVATIVES ARE STUN (NUTS).

HEBREW =HE-BE-OUR-EW. So, Boys were tossed to Crocodiles in Kemet. Mayans also Painted Kids Blue and threw them to Horrid Deaths, in Yucatan Wells.

PALACE =PEE-A-LACE, the USA makes up about 5% of the World's Population now. But a Quarter of all Global Prisoners are confined there for Live Display.

PRISON =PEE-OUR-IS-ON, and all people misdeeds are caused by Alien God's. So, we really should take time out to transcend pass these Devil Oppressions.

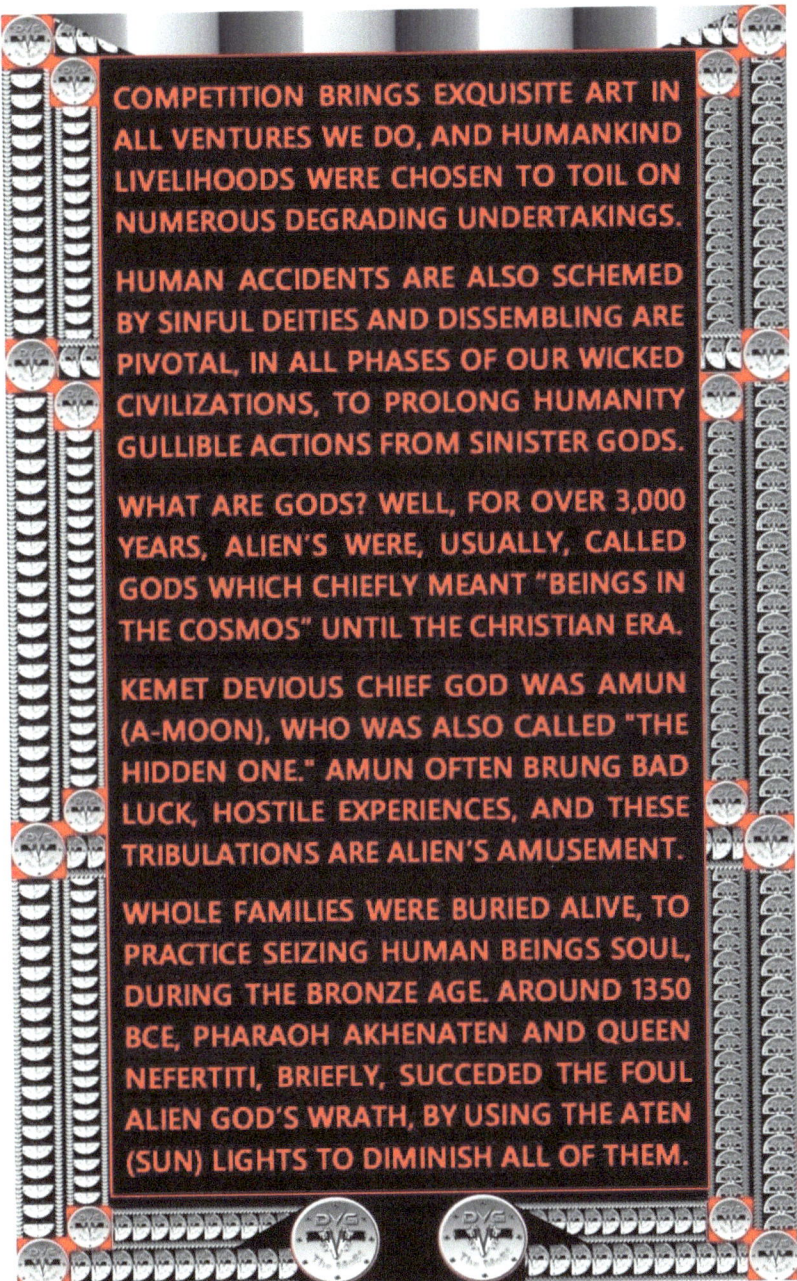

COMPETITION BRINGS EXQUISITE ART IN ALL VENTURES WE DO, AND HUMANKIND LIVELIHOODS WERE CHOSEN TO TOIL ON NUMEROUS DEGRADING UNDERTAKINGS.

HUMAN ACCIDENTS ARE ALSO SCHEMED BY SINFUL DEITIES AND DISSEMBLING ARE PIVOTAL, IN ALL PHASES OF OUR WICKED CIVILIZATIONS, TO PROLONG HUMANITY GULLIBLE ACTIONS FROM SINISTER GODS.

WHAT ARE GODS? WELL, FOR OVER 3,000 YEARS, ALIEN'S WERE, USUALLY, CALLED GODS WHICH CHIEFLY MEANT "BEINGS IN THE COSMOS" UNTIL THE CHRISTIAN ERA.

KEMET DEVIOUS CHIEF GOD WAS AMUN (A-MOON), WHO WAS ALSO CALLED "THE HIDDEN ONE." AMUN OFTEN BRUNG BAD LUCK, HOSTILE EXPERIENCES, AND THESE TRIBULATIONS ARE ALIEN'S AMUSEMENT.

WHOLE FAMILIES WERE BURIED ALIVE, TO PRACTICE SEIZING HUMAN BEINGS SOUL, DURING THE BRONZE AGE. AROUND 1350 BCE, PHARAOH AKHENATEN AND QUEEN NEFERTITI, BRIEFLY, SUCCEDED THE FOUL ALIEN GOD'S WRATH, BY USING THE ATEN (SUN) LIGHTS TO DIMINISH ALL OF THEM.

AKHENATEN
DVG
VICTORY

AKHENATEN AND NEFERTITI STAND, BY USING SUN PHOTONS, WITH OPEN QUARTERS, WERE HEROIC. BUT THEY COULDN'T COMPREHEND HOW PURE SUPER EC METALS DEGRADE OUR BODIES, AND MADE GODS MORE UBIQUITOUS.

SADLY, THEY KEPT UTILIZING EC GOLD DAILY, THIS LED INTO CIVIL WARS, PANDEMICS, AND ALSO THE DEMISE OF HUMANKIND'S REVIVAL.

ALIENS ALSO LIKE TO CRY. SO, OUR HISTORY IS FULL OF GREAT PEOPLE WHO, UNEXPECTEDLY, DIED, AND MANY FAMILIES SCREAMED WHY!

SADLY, EXTRATERRESTRIALS OFTEN BETRAYED AND ORGANIZED PEOPLE GRIEVING FATES, TO BROADEN THEIR DIRE BEREAVEMENT SHOWS.

MAINSTREAM CREATORS ALSO WONDER WHY GENIUSES, IN THE PAST, DIDN'T INVENT THEIR PRODUCT. BUT THIS IS A WALL (LAW) SCHEME.

HUMANS CREATE THINGS, WHEN THE TIME IS RIGHT, FOR GOD'S NEW-ER (NEWER) SCIENCE, AND IT'S CAUSED BY WHIZ-DUMB (WISDOM).

WE ARE MISLED TO LABOR ON ENDEAVOURS PEOPLE SHOULDN'T BE. WE CAN ALSO TRAVEL THE UNIVERSE SAFELY, JUST LIKE ALIEN'S ARE.

THIS CAN BE ACHIEVED FROM UTILIZING THE HIDDEN ONE TECHNOLOGY. SO, A SPACESHIP FOR INTERSTELLER SPACE TRAVEL IS OBSOLETE.

Persistence

HUMAN BEINGS SCIENCE IS A COMICAL PLEASURE FOR CLEVERER ALIEN GODS, AND WE'RE USING THE "CONTROL ELEMENT" GOLD PROTONS IN PARTICLE COLLIDERS! IT SEEMS THEY'RE PLAYING WITH FIRE, I LIKEN MOST SCIENCE TO BUILDING A SANDCASTLE, WHICH ARE UNMERITED AND OUTLANDISH TODAY.

CAN PEOPLE ACHIEVE LONGEVITY ON EARTH? OUR PLANETS NATURAL DISASTERS ARE TOO COMMON, AND PROLONG EXPOSER TO SUN RADIATION WILL LEAD TO CANCER CELLS. FURTHERMORE, RANDOM SPACE OBJECTS & HYPERNOVAS CAN ALSO KILL US.

THEREFORE, LIVING AWAY FROM DISASTER, WILL BE PEOPLE FIRST QUEST TO LIVE UNTHINKABLE AGES; THIS COULD BE ACHIEVED IN OUR SOLAR SYSTEM FROM LIVING INSIDE PROTOPLANETS, MOONS, OR ASTEROIDS BY US USING QUANTUM ENGINEERING ENVIRONMENTS, FOR PEOPLE HEALTH PERSISTENCE.

UNDOUBTEDLY, PRODUCING SIMULATED WORLDS FOR PERPLEX ENTERTAINMENT, SIMILAR TO A TUBE TECHNOLOGY, WILL BE PIVOTAL FOR EASING FOLKS SOLITARY LIFE. BUT RIDDING CON IS NEEDED FIRST.

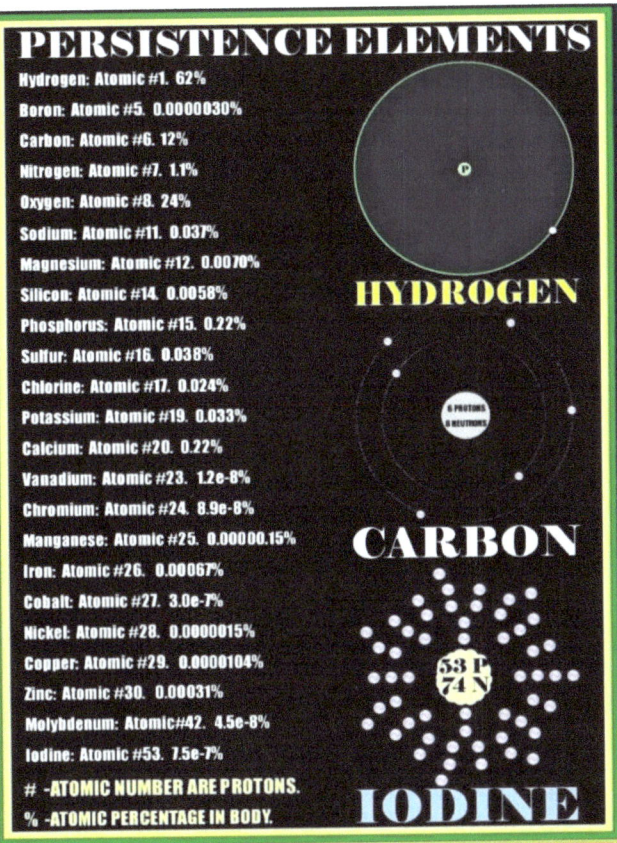

PERSISTENCE ELEMENTS

Hydrogen: Atomic #1. 62%

Boron: Atomic #5. 0.0000030%

Carbon: Atomic #6. 12%

Nitrogen: Atomic #7. 1.1%

Oxygen: Atomic #8. 24%

Sodium: Atomic #11. 0.037%

Magnesium: Atomic #12. 0.0070%

Silicon: Atomic #14. 0.0058%

Phosphorus: Atomic #15. 0.22%

Sulfur: Atomic #16. 0.038%

Chlorine: Atomic #17. 0.024%

Potassium: Atomic #19. 0.033%

Calcium: Atomic #20. 0.22%

Vanadium: Atomic #23. 1.2e-8%

Chromium: Atomic #24. 8.9e-8%

Manganese: Atomic #25. 0.00000.15%

Iron: Atomic #26. 0.00067%

Cobalt: Atomic #27. 3.0e-7%

Nickel: Atomic #28. 0.0000015%

Copper: Atomic #29. 0.0000104%

Zinc: Atomic #30. 0.00031%

Molybdenum: Atomic#42. 4.5e-8%

Iodine: Atomic #53. 7.5e-7%

-ATOMIC NUMBER ARE PROTONS.

% -ATOMIC PERCENTAGE IN BODY.

Health Persistence could be achieved by avoiding Elements people aren't made of like Lead, Mercury, and Gold. These Heavy Metals can backfire, while detoxing, because they're also over 7 times heavier than the average Human Body Atom; it's similar to Shooting an 80 Caliber Bullet through a 10 Caliber Barrel, and Demolition Organs like a Wrecking Ball. But Lead is in our Water Pipe System, and it leaches more, each time there's a break, in the City's Water Disperse, likened to Flint Michigan's Crisis in 2014.

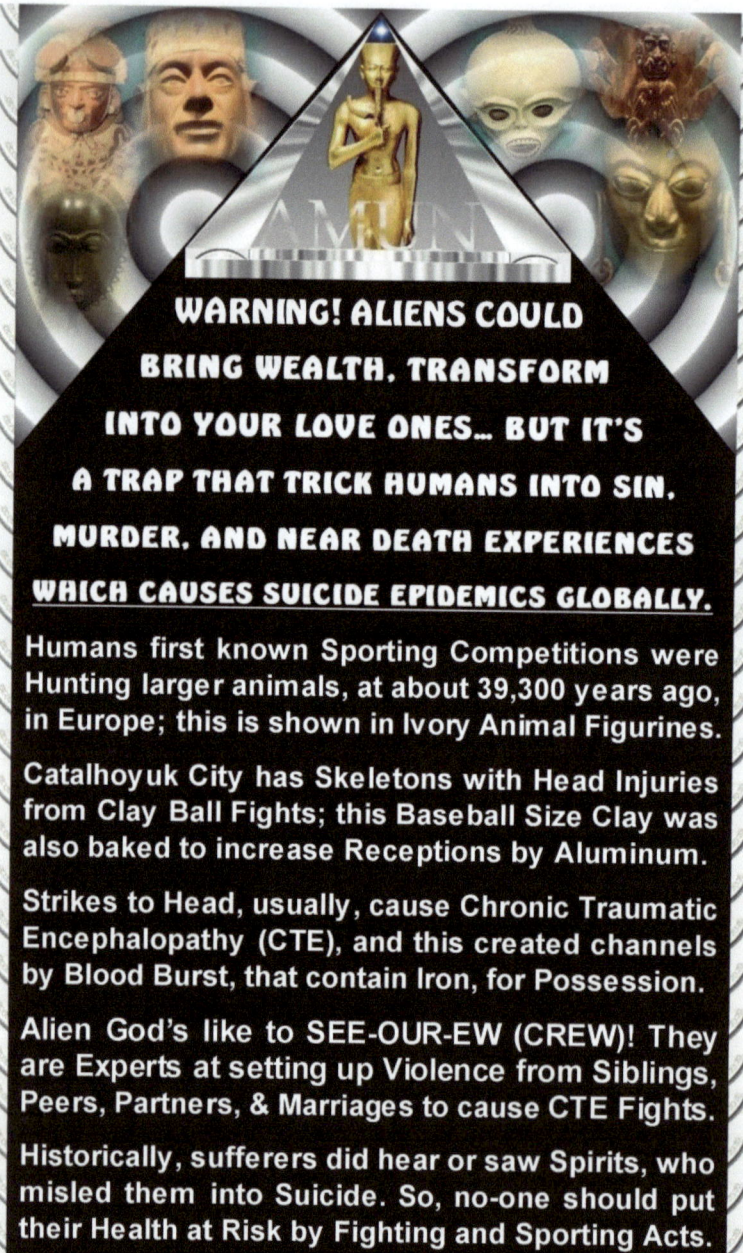

WARNING! ALIENS COULD BRING WEALTH, TRANSFORM INTO YOUR LOVE ONES… BUT IT'S A TRAP THAT TRICK HUMANS INTO SIN, MURDER, AND NEAR DEATH EXPERIENCES WHICH CAUSES SUICIDE EPIDEMICS GLOBALLY.

Humans first known Sporting Competitions were Hunting larger animals, at about 39,300 years ago, in Europe; this is shown in Ivory Animal Figurines.

Catalhoyuk City has Skeletons with Head Injuries from Clay Ball Fights; this Baseball Size Clay was also baked to increase Receptions by Aluminum.

Strikes to Head, usually, cause Chronic Traumatic Encephalopathy (CTE), and this created channels by Blood Burst, that contain Iron, for Possession.

Alien God's like to SEE-OUR-EW (CREW)! They are Experts at setting up Violence from Siblings, Peers, Partners, & Marriages to cause CTE Fights.

Historically, sufferers did hear or saw Spirits, who misled them into Suicide. So, no-one should put their Health at Risk by Fighting and Sporting Acts.

Before Aliens Engineered Epic Daredevil Gaming for Civilization Display, they first made more Characters of Races by using Diseases and Incest in Catalhoyuk. Humankind DNA suggest many relocated to Europe, along with their Animals, and also Built Stonehenge.

HOUSE =HOLE-USE. Catalhoyuk Bizarre Homes have no Doors and Roof Entries, like Test Tubes, designed to keep all the Poison accumulating inside. Residents also painted the Walls Monthly, with Red Ochre, and they're the best preserved Homes in Anatolia Turkey.

Smoke Stains, from Cooking, occurred inside these Houses. But this newer Plaster was done Monthly to likely keep the EC Iron Oxide (Red Ochre) Walls and Paintings fresh; they're likened to 360 degree Digital Video Cameras, when Quantum Engineering is prime.

HOME =HOLE-ME. Catalhoyuk Homes, where about 8,000 people lived at, are the most Dreadful Places, Folks Dwelled Inside, in likely Human Beings History.

FAMILIES =FAM-EYE-LIES. Ladders were also utilized for climbing inside Roof Entries, because they're no streets. So, Catalhoyuk Dwellings were built closer to each other, and people walked on the Rooftops daily.

ATROCITY =CITY of Catalhoyuk Houses, that date to around 7100-5700 BCE. This is the most Sick-making and frightening City! Dozens of decomposing Bodies were buried in them by using Red Ochre, and some had Beads of Teeth that accumulated Toxic Air inside.

Catalhoyuk City Viruses would've caused damage in folks Immune System, and branched out into Bloody Channels, that also increased Alien God's Reception.

DWELLER =DE-WELL-ER. Grim Microorganisms and Decomposition Methane Gases would've often been extreme for Dwellers. Sadly, thousands lived in these Homes for well over a century before, mysteriously, burying them, and building new Houses on top of it.

Black Mold Exposer, from the Homes Roof Openings was, definitely, also higher. Fouler smells by, literally, Living on a Landfill full of Decomposing Bodies and Sewage, would've made the City Proximity Atrocious.

LUPUS =LOOP-US. Neolithic Fertile Crescent Cities like Catalhoyuk are Very Sad to see; these Monstrous Oppressions led to over 90% of all Deadly Diseases, & Heavy Metal Toxicity, Humans still lives with today.

ASPHALT =ASS-FAULT to naive people utilizing toxic Benzene Chemicals, on Earth Roads, proven to cause Cancer. HAIR ANALYST TEST can work superior when testing Heavy Metal Levels, Chemicals, and people should frequently use natural remedies for Detoxing.

SLAVERY =SLAY-VERY. It seems Slaves first toiled as Gold Miners, and this also led to Cotton, because it's a Super EC Material. So, Edison and Swan used it for the first Incandescent Light Bulbs, Patented in 1879.

Moreover, Rechargeable Car Batteries, utilizing Pure Silver Cylinders, are also using Superior Cotton now. Sadly, CON Wealth is thriving and we should Insight...

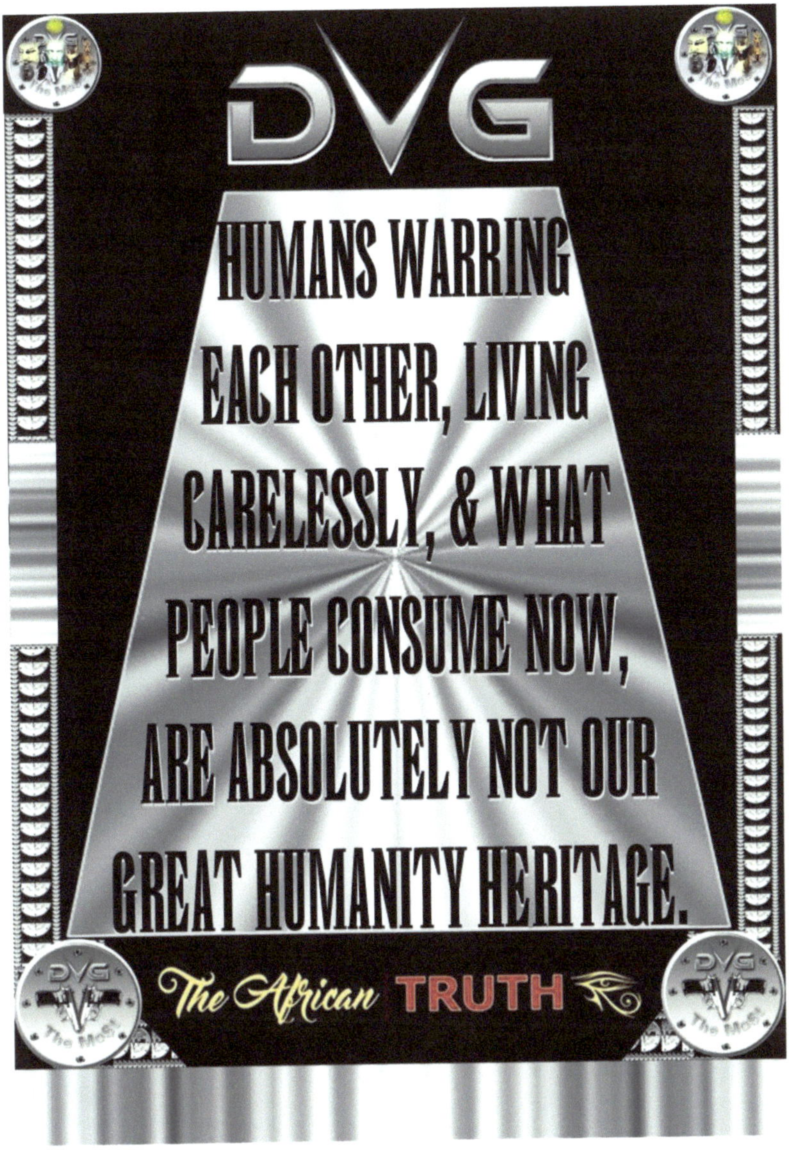
DVG
HUMANS WARRING
EACH OTHER, LIVING
CARELESSLY, & WHAT
PEOPLE CONSUME NOW,
ARE ABSOLUTELY NOT OUR
GREAT HUMANITY HERITAGE.
The African TRUTH

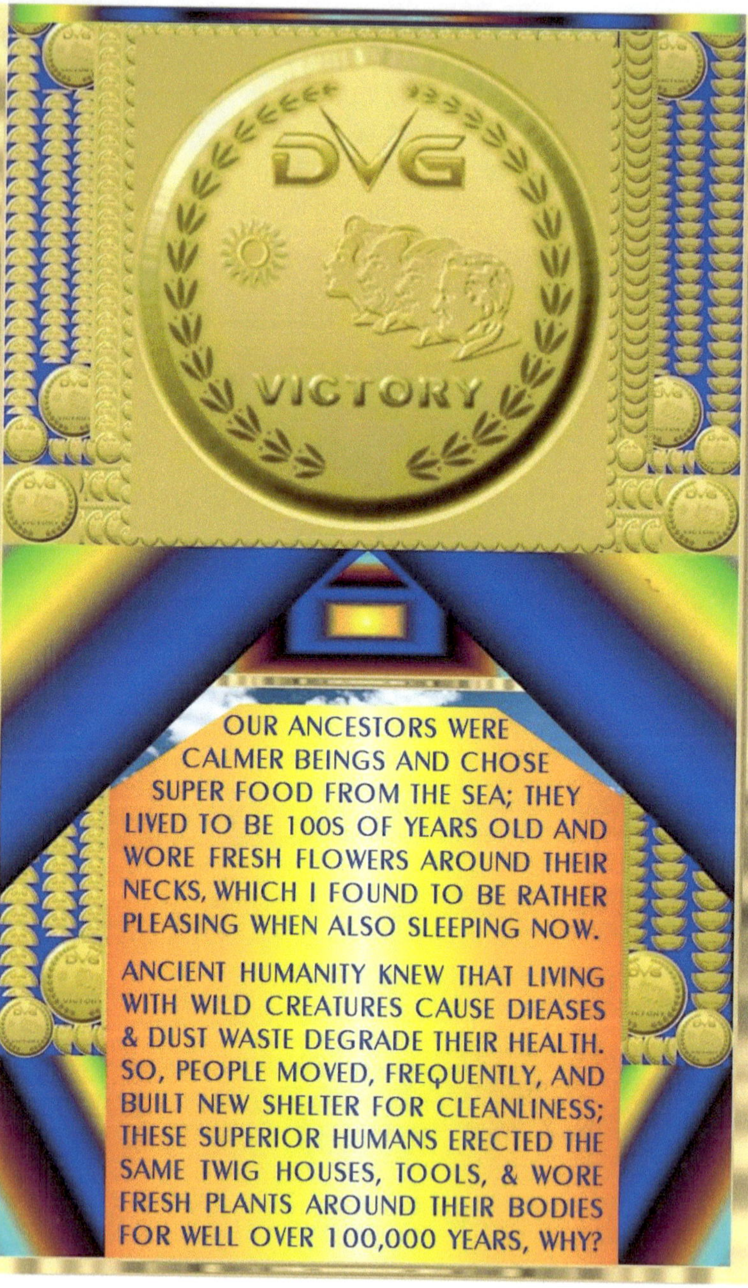

OUR ANCESTORS WERE CALMER BEINGS AND CHOSE SUPER FOOD FROM THE SEA; THEY LIVED TO BE 100S OF YEARS OLD AND WORE FRESH FLOWERS AROUND THEIR NECKS, WHICH I FOUND TO BE RATHER PLEASING WHEN ALSO SLEEPING NOW.

ANCIENT HUMANITY KNEW THAT LIVING WITH WILD CREATURES CAUSE DIEASES & DUST WASTE DEGRADE THEIR HEALTH. SO, PEOPLE MOVED, FREQUENTLY, AND BUILT NEW SHELTER FOR CLEANLINESS; THESE SUPERIOR HUMANS ERECTED THE SAME TWIG HOUSES, TOOLS, & WORE FRESH PLANTS AROUND THEIR BODIES FOR WELL OVER 100,000 YEARS, WHY?

VICTORY
VICTORY
DVG
PERSISTENCE
Persistence
SAN PEOPLE PEERLESS HEALTH
PERSISTENCE STAYS THE SAME
AND DEGRADERS ALWAYS CHANGE.
The African TRUTH

THE AFRICAN TRUTH.

Today, the DEMOLITION-INSIDE (DEMON) folks have us Programmed to choose Byproducts that Shortens Humankind's Lifespan. But the Brightest People don't wear EC Attire laced with Chemicals.

BRIGHT =BE-RIGHT folks, and they're our earliest Human Beings, living inside Africa, called the San and we're being duped to call them BUSH PEOPLE.

But they once lived to be hundreds of years old, and the San doesn't Domesticate Animals, why? Living with Creatures caused the Direst Diseases, folks still live with, and lure Predators in Wildlife.

Human African Ancestors utilized Natural Wood like Olive Trees, for their Homes, which is one of the best Natural Remedies for Cold Viruses; they also used Edible Plants over Wooden Fires, when Cooking, and are still Superior Nomadic Thinkers.

PACKAGE =PACK-AGE. So, many Bad Goods like Styrofoam and Plastics are, actually, designed to Leach Poison in Food, Humans Eat or Drink daily; the San use Ostrich Eggs to store Drinking Water.

PLASTIC =PEE-LAST-I-SEE, in our Body & Oceans! The Lethal Microplastics are Poisoning the Earth, horribly, and Humans should rise above this CON.

THE AFRICAN TRUTH.

BE-ER (BEER) and BE-READ (BREAD) were made with Pottery for increasing Aliens Reception from Aluminum, which Leached more with each usage.

Historically, Human Beings chiefly lived off Africa Lakes and Coastlines, close to the Equator, where our Weather is more Stable with Ultraviolet Light from our Sun; the Sunrays also makes Vitamin D and pushes Toxins out of our Bodies more rapidly.

The Stellar San folks still mostly live similar to our Ancestors; they also move often and doesn't like to DE-WELL (DWELL) in most Permanent Homes, which Accumulates Dust Waste from our bodies.

The San often Hunts, for Fresher Food, every day, and use Natural Goods over their body; they also have no Chiefs, and choose to be Peaceful Beings.

Today, Governments are Insisting Modernization to the San People, which is degrading this most Ancient Nomadic faster. Stations serving Alcohol are causing Drunkenness, Strife, Depression, and now Families are sadly breaking up rapidly today.

San People are MISS-FOR-TUNE (MISFORTUNE), and an example of what occurred to Humankind, during Gods Birth of Civilization, 5,500 years ago.

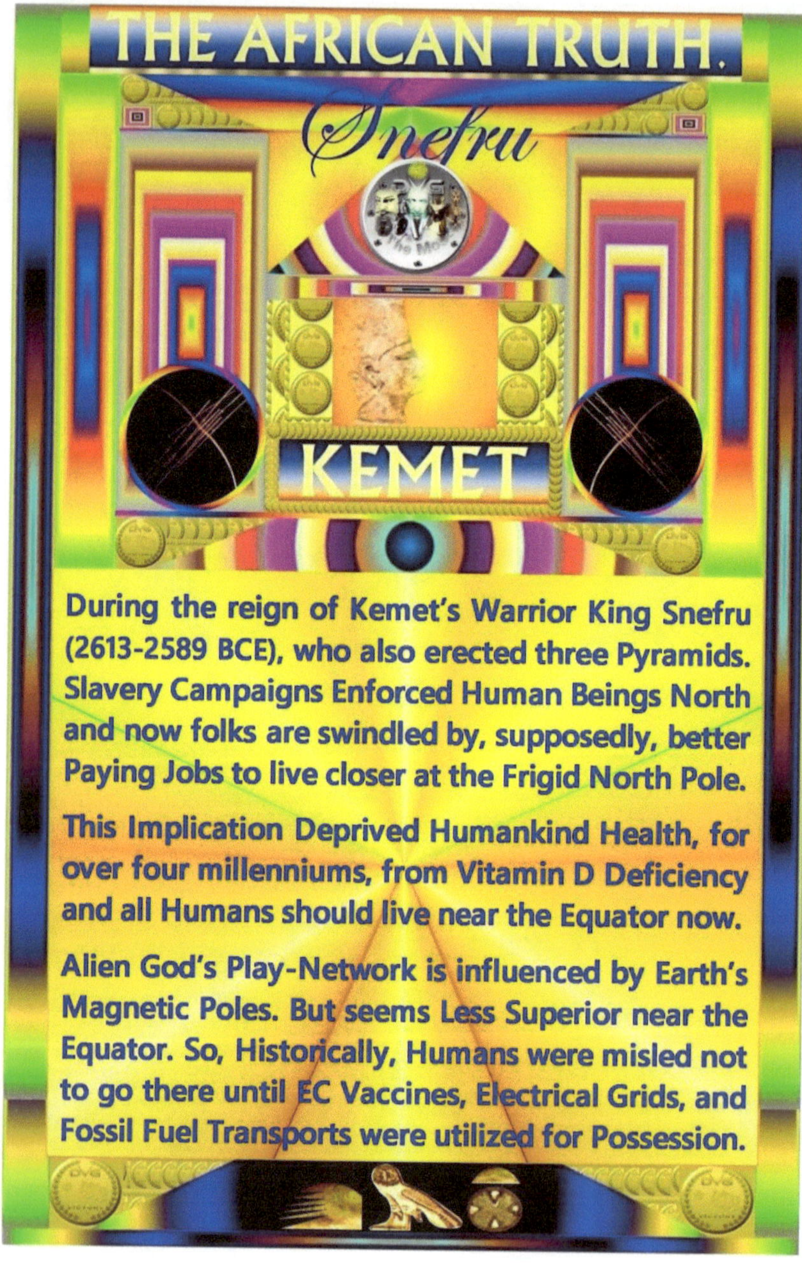
THE AFRICAN TRUTH.
Snefru
KEMET
During the reign of Kemet's Warrior King Snefru (2613-2589 BCE), who also erected three Pyramids. Slavery Campaigns Enforced Human Beings North and now folks are swindled by, supposedly, better Paying Jobs to live closer at the Frigid North Pole.
This Implication Deprived Humankind Health, for over four millenniums, from Vitamin D Deficiency and all Humans should live near the Equator now.
Alien God's Play-Network is influenced by Earth's Magnetic Poles. But seems Less Superior near the Equator. So, Historically, Humans were misled not to go there until EC Vaccines, Electrical Grids, and Fossil Fuel Transports were utilized for Possession.

RECORD = "WRECK ORDINANCE."

Wreck Ordinance effect entertainers, politicians, athletes, friends, families, & car accidents, caused on the highway, are all conspired for more epic dehumanization scenes. Since Roman times, a gladiator was a star that =rats, why? WHO-MAN-BEING Trials & Tribulations are beloved by Gods.

THE SLICK DUPE.

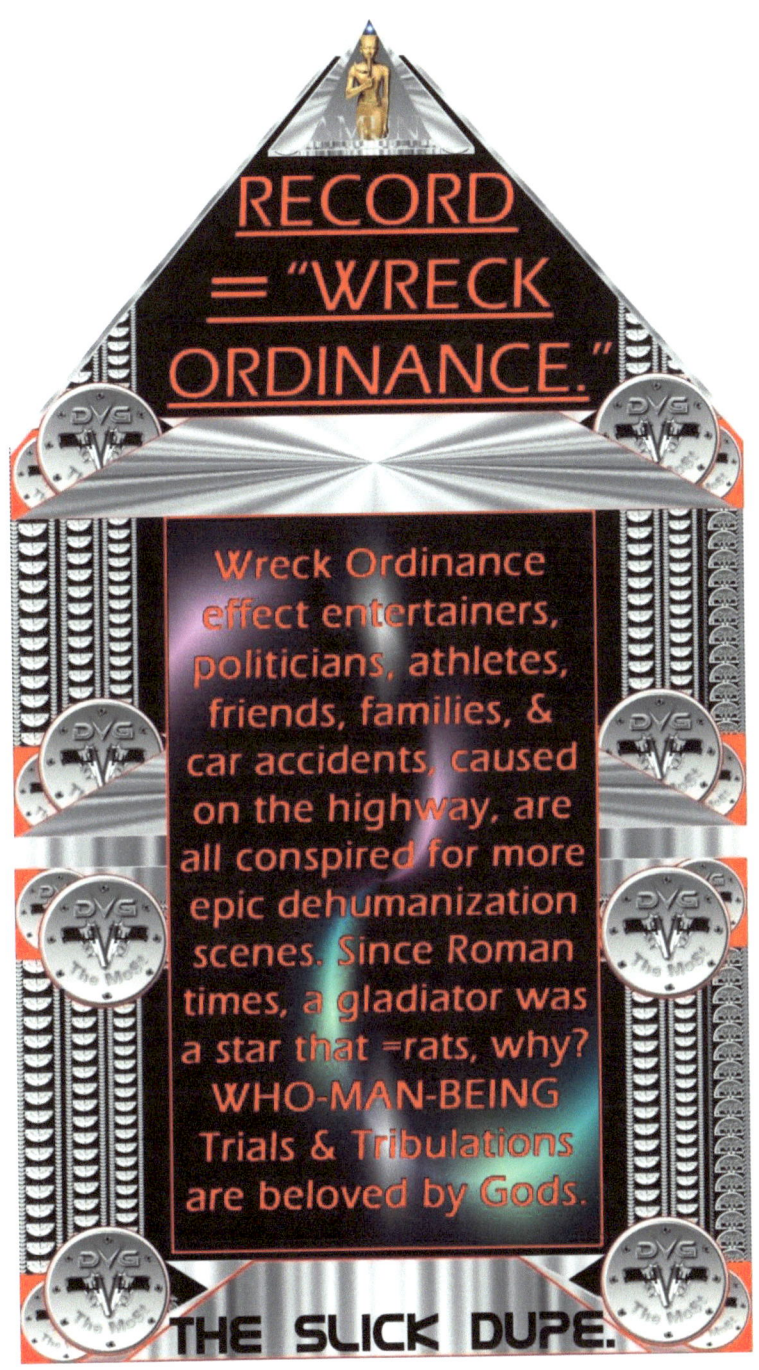

Micro-deception is making us perceive people are advancing in Technology, to make our Lives more Accessible, today.

But Transports, Factories, and Farming increases Pollution for Live Receptions, SILVER-WEAR (SILVERWARE) does also.

Useless Transport Gasoline Engines are increasing Carbon Dioxide to sad Earth Levels not seen in Twenty Million Years!

This is Plotted for Programming People Pathological. Industrial Amalgamation, from earlier Mining, have also released Lead Metals in Earth's Atmosphere, and this was proven from Ice-core Samples.

Alcohol and Drugs make us MORE-ON (MORON) to Stark Micro-deception, by Increasing DOPE-A-MEN (DOPAMINE).

THE SLICK DUPE.

The Mammal, which Human Beings Religiously Cherished the most, is producing Osteoporosis causing Milk, that contains the most Opioids, of all known Animals, called Beta-Casomorphin 7.

Unfortunately, this is why deceptive Cow Milk is still number-one, and also used by Aliens Prime, to increase Dopamine inside our bodies, today.

REPENT =RE-PEE-ENTERTAINMENT, and Aliens Desire the Most! This can be seen by maximum numbers of Human Being Experiences on Earth.

Aliens Envy Sex Thrills, War Kills, Violent Rants, Injustice, and Big City Gangster Life. Sadly, this Plot is recurring in numbers of Beatings, Rapes, Murders, Terrors, and Wars for Displays yearly!

Alien's like to cover their History of Oppression, for preventing us from rediscovering the Truth. Kemet Medu Neter Language was repressed for 1500 years, till finding the Rosetta Stone in 1799.

Africa's oldest known Civilization was called Ta-Seti (KUSH). A fake Lake Nasser, chiefly, has this covered now, and it's caused by the Aswan Dam.

NASSER =INSIDE-ASS-ER. Ta-Seti's Afro African History is being hindered by Alien's. The Nilo-Saharans Fort Cities seems to have Intellectuals Archived, and this needs to stay buried in Sudan.

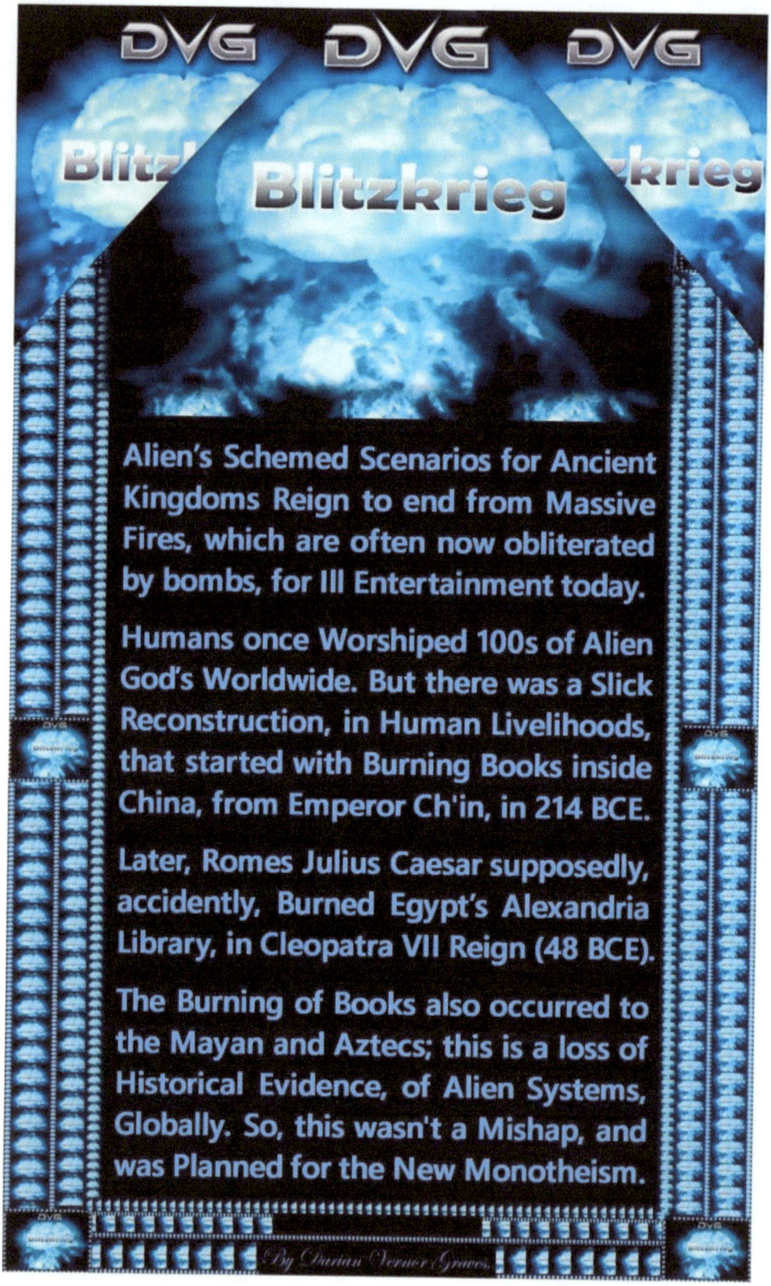
DVG DVG DVG
Blitzkrieg
Alien's Schemed Scenarios for Ancient Kingdoms Reign to end from Massive Fires, which are often now obliterated by bombs, for Ill Entertainment today.
Humans once Worshiped 100s of Alien God's Worldwide. But there was a Slick Reconstruction, in Human Livelihoods, that started with Burning Books inside China, from Emperor Ch'in, in 214 BCE.
Later, Romes Julius Caesar supposedly, accidently, Burned Egypt's Alexandria Library, in Cleopatra VII Reign (48 BCE).
The Burning of Books also occurred to the Mayan and Aztecs; this is a loss of Historical Evidence, of Alien Systems, Globally. So, this wasn't a Mishap, and was Planned for the New Monotheism.
By Darian Vernor Graves

MICROECONOMICS.

Mercury Vaccinated Children, mostly, Hear or Vision Alien God's during their Lives. But Folk shouldn't Hear, See, and Sense Abnormal Entities; this can also be Rid by Reducing EC Metals inside our Bodies.

THE SEAT OF HUMAN SOULS are Bones and Hearts. During Eerily Mummification, Priests took our Brains out through the Nose and Disposed them.

But SILVER and GOLD in our Livers, Intestines, and Lungs were Secured Inside Canopic Jars for Kemet's Dog Anubis.

Eureka, these are clearly why Cemeteries have Bad Portals, Globally, because they Store Soul Treasure that's Beloved.

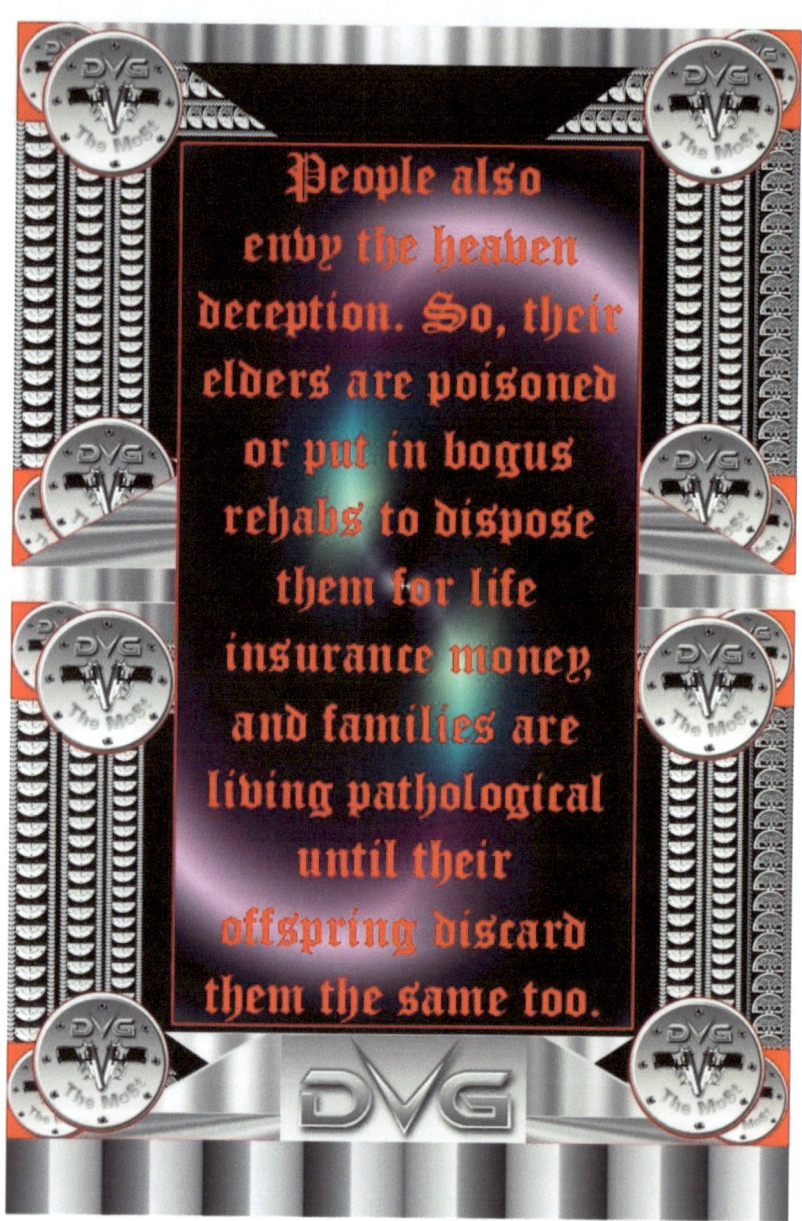

People also envy the heaven deception. So, their elders are poisoned or put in bogus rehabs to dispose them for life insurance money, and families are living pathological until their offspring discard them the same too.

Inheritance and Life Insurance Policies Increase Human odds of being Murdered, in their Primes, 1000 times. So, don't leave Substantial Amounts of Money to anyone, and Teach your Dependents how to be Self-sufficient for Optimizing their Life.

Seniors Disposed by their Children are an Agenda that many Kings and Queens fell Victim from. In-fact, it's influenced more than ever today, why? Humankind can live Unthinkable Ages. But sadly, Aliens don't Desire Possessing Elders for Rapture.

Kemetics said "Mut (Moot) is Amun's Wife and is the Grandmother of all the Gods." Mut Acts like the Enforcer, for Micro-deception, and can bring, supposedly, Good Fortunes to Humans every day.

ANGEL =A-INSIDE-GEL. Bright Lights, which also disrupt our Eyes and Video Cameras have similar effects on Alien WATCHERS (WATCH-ER). So, Light is decreasing Extraterrestrial Possession Contacts.

This is why God's are still fond of Night, and kept Civilization in the Dark, for 5,300 years. But Plan to Rid our Modernism by insisting a Nuclear War! We are definitely Living in a Brief Series, which is Schemed to be Demolished for their Gratification.

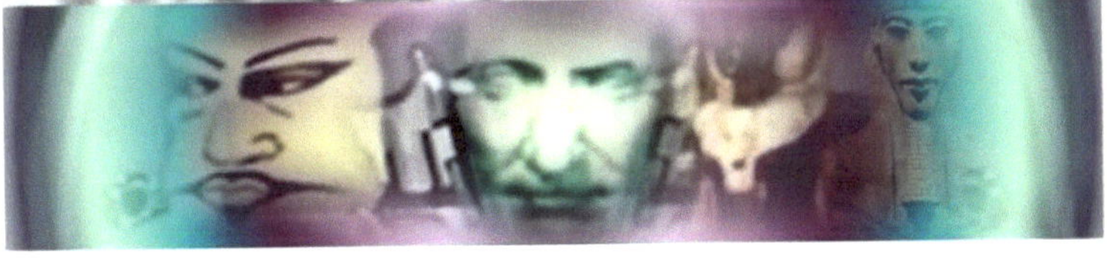

MICRODECEPTION

Today, most people don't recollect how Perilous Dust Particles are Shining in a House Sunlight. Everything inside Dwellings, Transports, Clothing, and Currencies Leaches in Air we Breathe, which Coalesce in Organs.

The FUR-INSIDE-ACE (FURNACE) Leach Pure Copper, Aluminum, and Chemicals in Dwellings. So, Living in the Bitter Cold, with Toxic Utilities, should be avoided.

COPPER is the COP and MASTER CONTROL ELEMENT, with over 2 Billion Metric Tons used in History; this is 1000 times more than Silver and Gold combined, at 2 Million Metric Tons. Unsuitable Computers, Fans, TVs, and Light Bulbs also Leaches Copper inside Dwellings.

Treated-Wood Products are often Micronized Copper Laced with the Toxic Arsenic! Leather Clothing, Belts, Shoes, Bags, Hats, Car Seats, and Furniture, Humans spends the most time on, are also made with Copper.

Treated-Wood Kitchen Cabinets and Utensils, that we Eat from, also contain Micronized Copper. In-fact, just putting Attire inside Copper-Wood Dressers Leaches in them too! So, Insight today, this isn't a Conjecture.

THE WOLF (FLOW) IS HERE! I tested all these Copper Products, that are also Poisoning Humans Health like Paints and Cookware. But chiefly designed for raising Live Receptions and why Aliens call them Possessions.

The Sixth Highest EC Element is Nickel (EC 22%), and Copper has 100% EC. Silver Coins were also utilized for Anti-Bacterial Purposes in Cups and Ship Hulls. Unfortunately, it caused Blue Veins overtime and Certain Chronic Health from Users.

Copper is Assembled for Pipelines to Leach into Drinking and Bathing Water Worldwide; it's also in the most abundant Coin, called the Penny, for Increasing Aliens Live Reception in people daily.

FIREWORKS =FIRE-WORKS, by raising Aliens Live Receptions. So, Ancient Cities were also burned often, which had EC Metals. Silver Cloud Seeding Flares, Transports, Electrical Grids, and Warheads have now made Ancient Gratifications Obsolete.

BE-LAST (BLAST) folks explode over 100,000 tons of Fireworks over people heads yearly; they Burn in Signature EC Element Colors: Like Aluminum silver, Copper blue, Barium green, Magnesium white, Sodium yellow, and Lithium red for Show.

Over 62% of a Human Body Atoms is only made of Hydrogen. But its Pure Form will Burn a Hole in Peoples Skin. So, don't BE-LAST (BLAST) folks.

Furthermore, all Pure Elements will Cause Harm to Humanity Bodies. So, Fireworks being Blasted should be Abolished for Optimum Health today.

Today, Humankind doesn't realize Mainstream Attire isn't produced to make Humans Look or Feel Good. Historically, Alien Gods dispersed all Clothing to Increase their Live Reception inside us, and this often Poisons Human Beings Health.

Clothing also mostly contain Toxic Inks which is absorbed by Humans Largest Organ, that is the Skin, and goes straight into people Bloodstream.

Clothing Confine Inessentials, leaving our Body, which can build up in Organs and cause Cancer. So, we should wear less Clothing with Materials like Hemp, Linen, Bamboo, and avoid Chemicals.

ITIS =IT-IS Deadly! Metals consumed coalesce in Organs, Bones, and causes Chronic Diseases. Deadly Heavy EC Elements increase the Watts, in our Body, and cause –ITIS (INFLAMMATION).

Pure EC Metals are also dim Batteries Leaching from our Cookware, Jewelry, and Vaccines that pull like Magnets in the Cardiovascular System.

Slavery was made possible from Leaders of Men Swindled to Mine Gold for Alien God's Display, which persists. Slavery Captives often Toiled on numerous other Sad Goods that are Toxic, and Cotton Clothing is also Bad for our Health, why?

COTTON CLOTHING, STEADY, LEACHES THE MOST BALLS OF CHEMICAL DYES, LACED WITH EC METALS & MICROBES, FROM ALL MAINSTREAM FABRICS, I TESTED, TODAY.

BELOW, THIS LAVISH CIVIL WAR ERA DRESS IS MADE OF SILK FABRIC. BUT, IT'S DYED WITH COPPER ARSENITE LIKE FURNISHINGS.

WHENEVER IT RAINED, THIS DEVIOUS DRESS POISONED WEARERS AND SWEAT WOULD'VE ALSO PULLED ARSENIC INSIDE THEIR BODY.

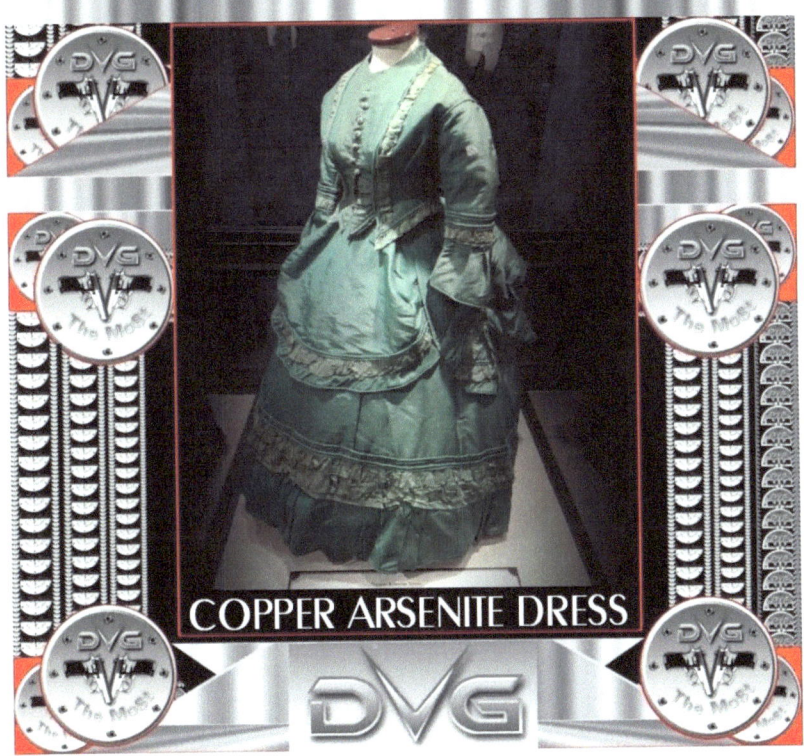

COPPER ARSENITE DRESS

DVG

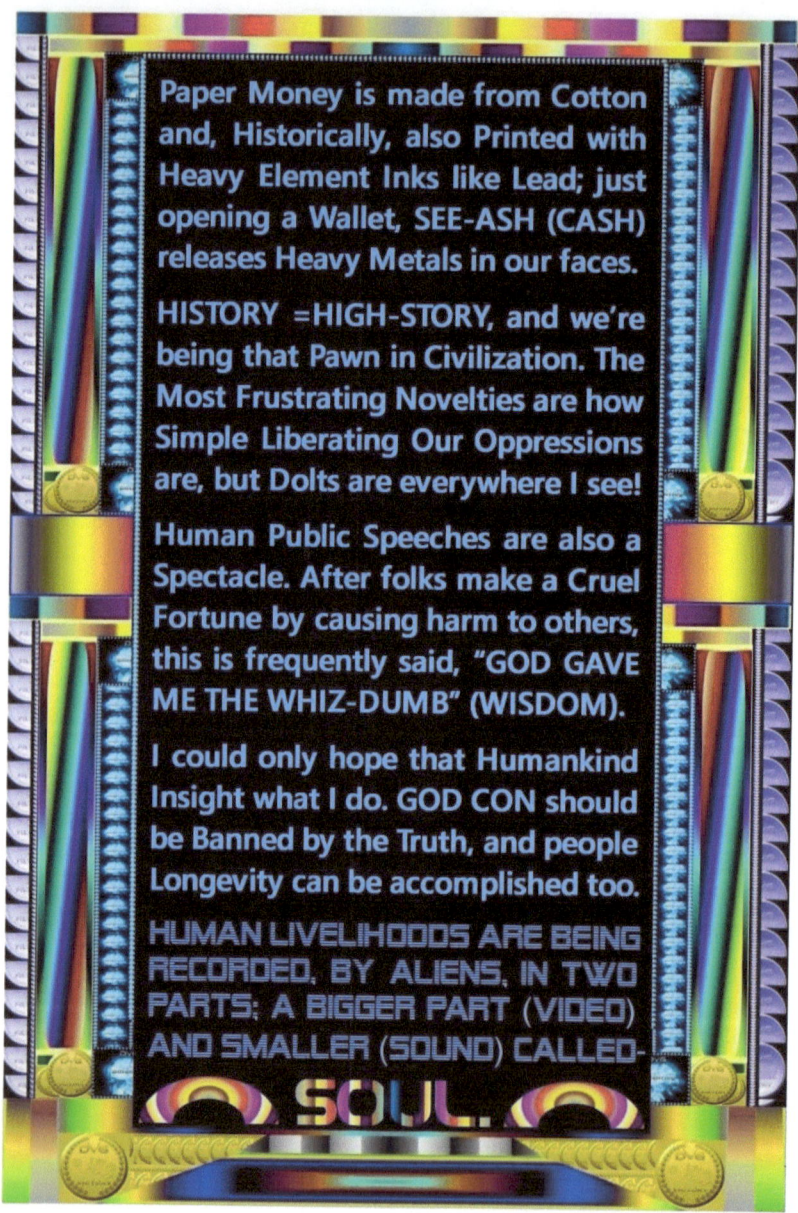

Paper Money is made from Cotton and, Historically, also Printed with Heavy Element Inks like Lead; just opening a Wallet, SEE-ASH (CASH) releases Heavy Metals in our faces.

HISTORY =HIGH-STORY, and we're being that Pawn in Civilization. The Most Frustrating Novelties are how Simple Liberating Our Oppressions are, but Dolts are everywhere I see!

Human Public Speeches are also a Spectacle. After folks make a Cruel Fortune by causing harm to others, this is frequently said, "GOD GAVE ME THE WHIZ-DUMB" (WISDOM).

I could only hope that Humankind Insight what I do. GOD CON should be Banned by the Truth, and people Longevity can be accomplished too.

HUMAN LIVELIHOODS ARE BEING RECORDED, BY ALIENS, IN TWO PARTS; A BIGGER PART (VIDEO) AND SMALLER (SOUND) CALLED-

SOUL.

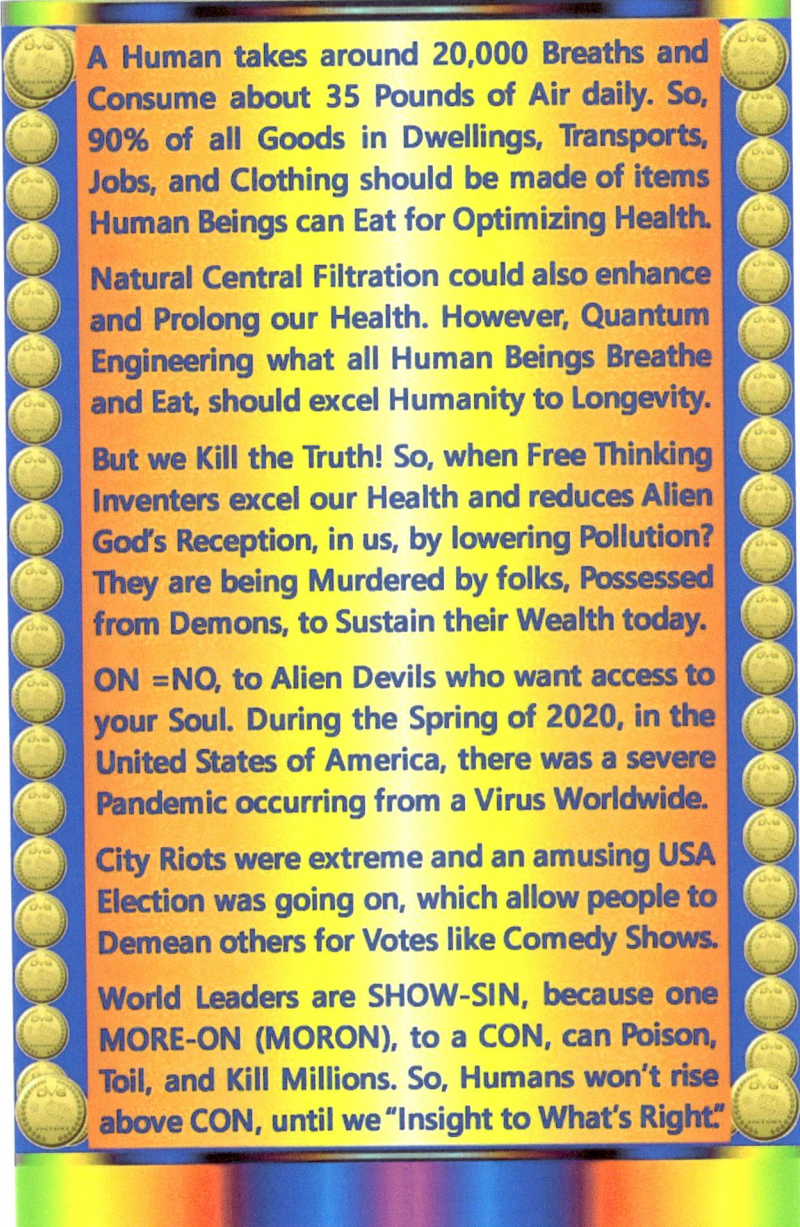

A Human takes around 20,000 Breaths and Consume about 35 Pounds of Air daily. So, 90% of all Goods in Dwellings, Transports, Jobs, and Clothing should be made of items Human Beings can Eat for Optimizing Health.

Natural Central Filtration could also enhance and Prolong our Health. However, Quantum Engineering what all Human Beings Breathe and Eat, should excel Humanity to Longevity.

But we Kill the Truth! So, when Free Thinking Inventers excel our Health and reduces Alien God's Reception, in us, by lowering Pollution? They are being Murdered by folks, Possessed from Demons, to Sustain their Wealth today.

ON =NO, to Alien Devils who want access to your Soul. During the Spring of 2020, in the United States of America, there was a severe Pandemic occurring from a Virus Worldwide.

City Riots were extreme and an amusing USA Election was going on, which allow people to Demean others for Votes like Comedy Shows.

World Leaders are SHOW-SIN, because one MORE-ON (MORON), to a CON, can Poison, Toil, and Kill Millions. So, Humans won't rise above CON, until we "Insight to What's Right."

RIOT CONTENTION HAVE BEEN RECURRING TO PEOPLE SINCE ANCIENT TIMES AND SUMERIA, FREQUENTLY, WOKE TO KILLED BODIES SPILLING BLOOD LIKE HOT BRONZE IN THE MOLTEN. TODAY, HUMANITY LIVE TO DIE FOR FILTHY MONEY, SEX, AND WINNING. BUT, HUMAN BEINGS SHOULD NEVER CONTEMPLATE THESE NAIVE THOUGHTS DAILY.

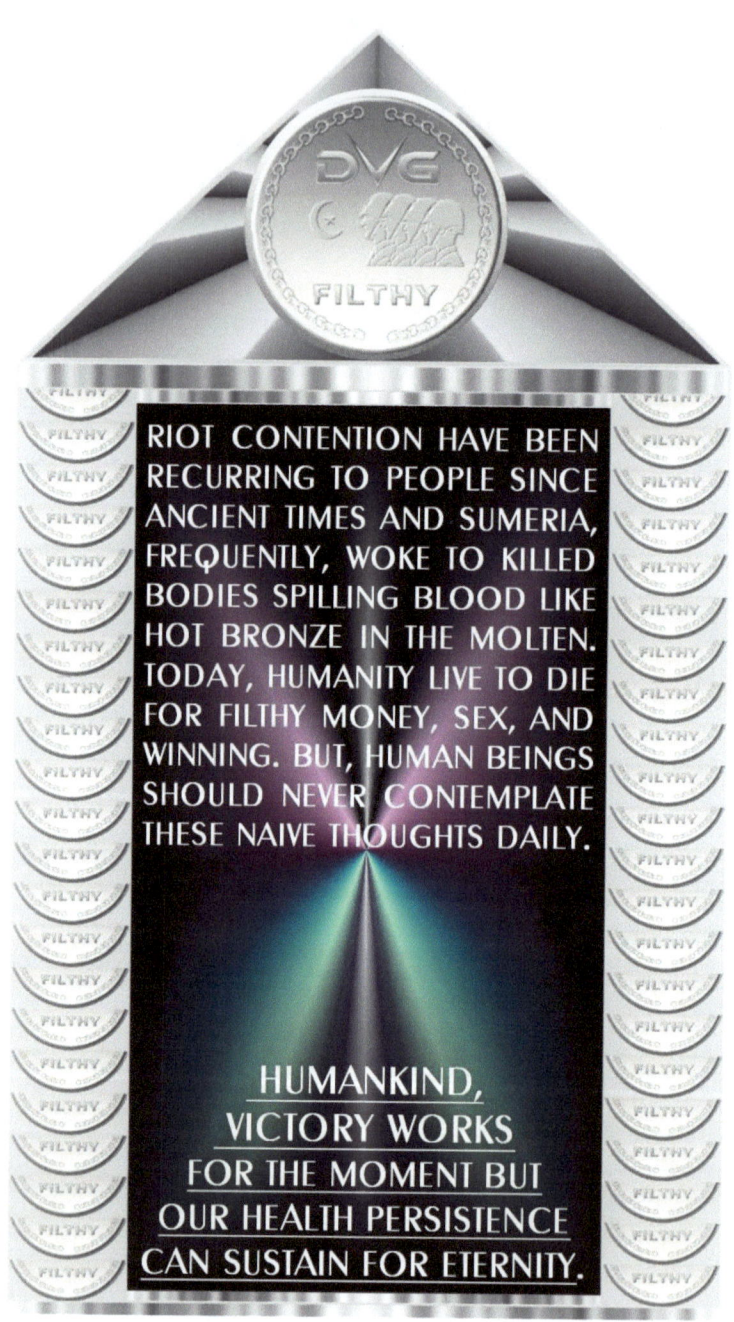

HUMANKIND,
VICTORY WORKS
FOR THE MOMENT BUT
OUR HEALTH PERSISTENCE
CAN SUSTAIN FOR ETERNITY.

RACISM

RACISM IS A PROGRAM FOR LIVE WAR-RANT EXPERIENCES DAILY. ANCIENT CITIES WERE BURNED TO THE GROUND OFTEN, BY CONSPIRED PREJUDICE TRENDS, THAT STILL PERSISTS.

All Dogs come from Wolves 13,000 Years Ago, the biggest dissimilarity is the Wolf could take care of itself and Trounce Dog Competitions. This is likened to Human Beings, but Racism also keep us all from returning to Superior Afro Africans, that Adapted Stellar Abilities for Longevity, which I'll explain later.

WAR

IS A LUCRATIVE

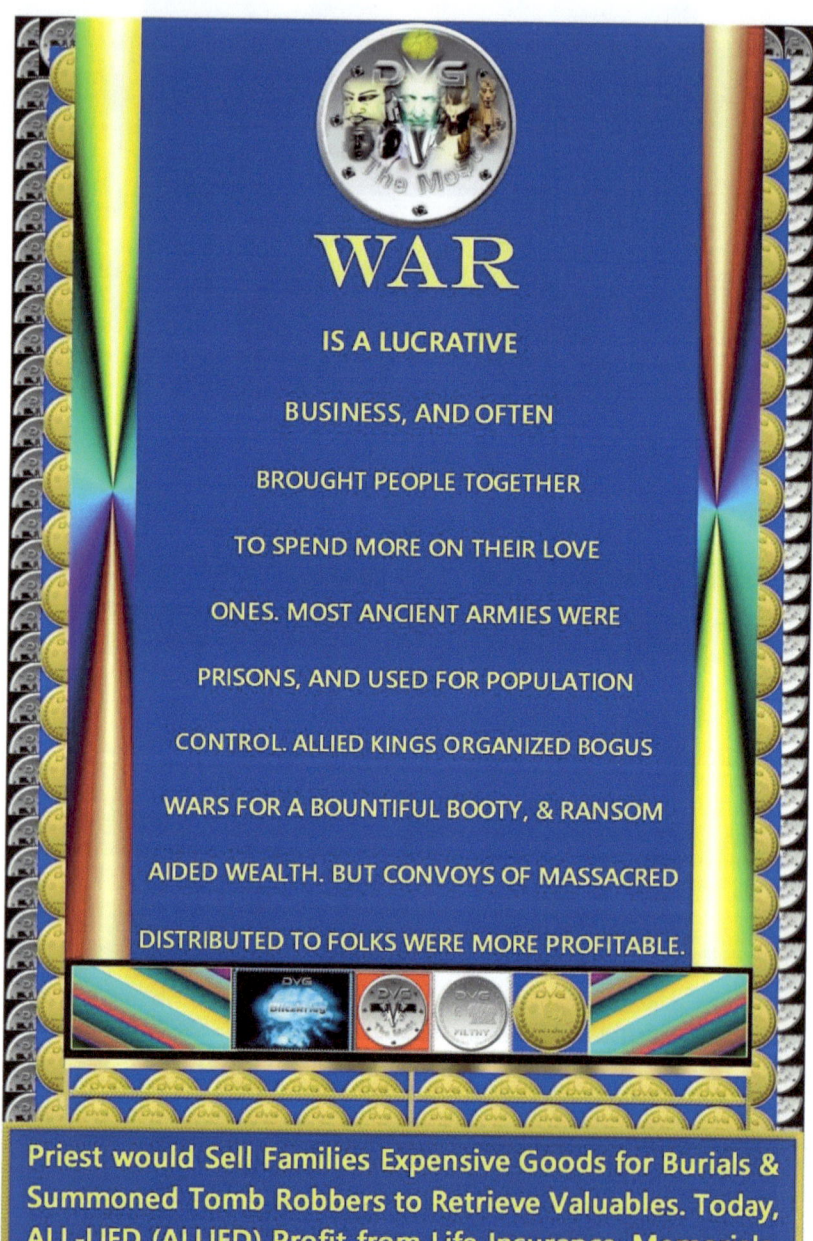

BUSINESS, AND OFTEN

BROUGHT PEOPLE TOGETHER

TO SPEND MORE ON THEIR LOVE

ONES. MOST ANCIENT ARMIES WERE

PRISONS, AND USED FOR POPULATION

CONTROL. ALLIED KINGS ORGANIZED BOGUS

WARS FOR A BOUNTIFUL BOOTY, & RANSOM

AIDED WEALTH. BUT CONVOYS OF MASSACRED

DISTRIBUTED TO FOLKS WERE MORE PROFITABLE.

Priest would Sell Families Expensive Goods for Burials & Summoned Tomb Robbers to Retrieve Valuables. Today, ALL-LIED (ALLIED) Profit from Life Insurance, Memorials, and utilizing Probate Courts to Redeem Dead Valuables.

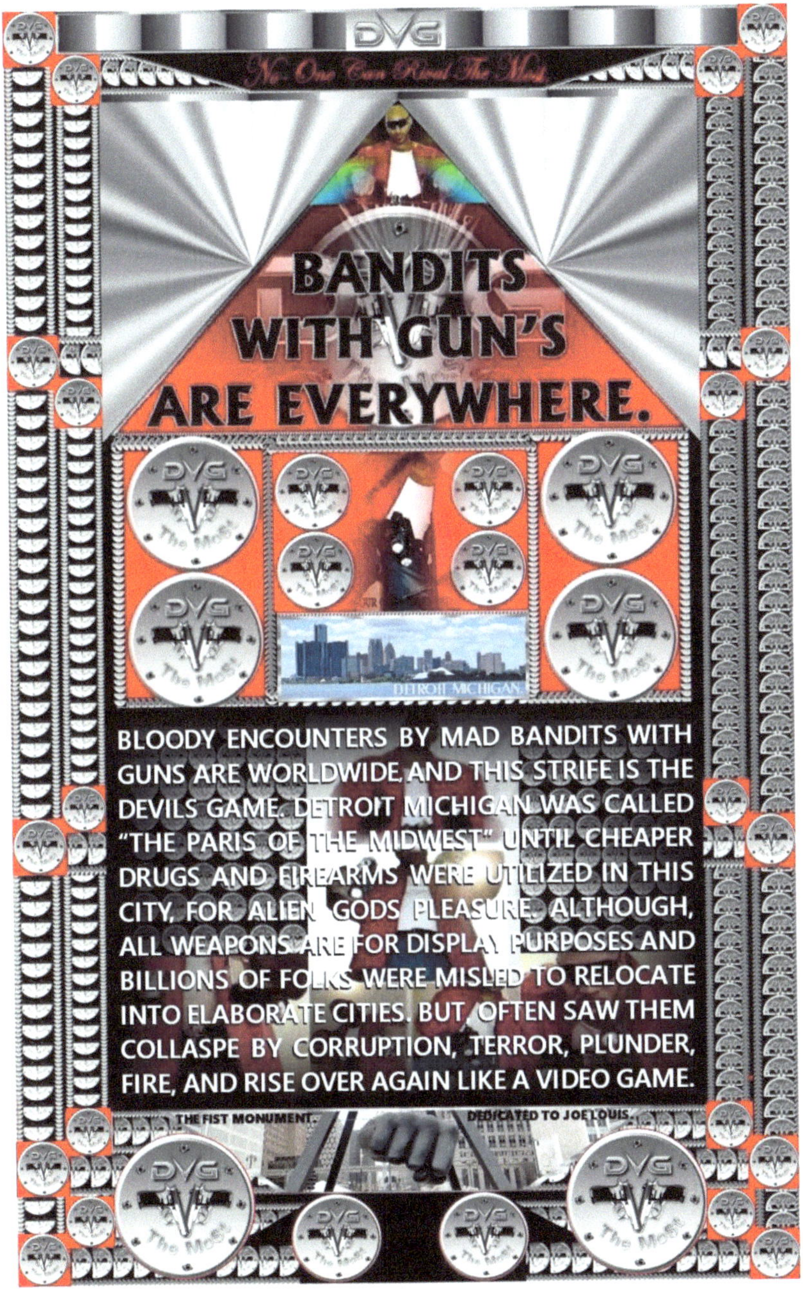

DVG
No One Can Rival The Most
BANDITS WITH GUN'S ARE EVERYWHERE.
DVG The Most
DETROIT MICHIGAN.
BLOODY ENCOUNTERS BY MAD BANDITS WITH GUNS ARE WORLDWIDE AND THIS STRIFE IS THE DEVILS GAME. DETROIT MICHIGAN WAS CALLED "THE PARIS OF THE MIDWEST" UNTIL CHEAPER DRUGS AND FIREARMS WERE UTILIZED IN THIS CITY, FOR ALIEN GODS PLEASURE. ALTHOUGH, ALL WEAPONS ARE FOR DISPLAY PURPOSES AND BILLIONS OF FOLKS WERE MISLED TO RELOCATE INTO ELABORATE CITIES. BUT, OFTEN SAW THEM COLLASPE BY CORRUPTION, TERROR, PLUNDER, FIRE, AND RISE OVER AGAIN LIKE A VIDEO GAME.
THE FIST MONUMENT.
DEDICATED TO JOE LOUIS.

WEAPON =WEPT-ON.

WAR =RAW (OUR-AW) @ RITUAL =WRIT-YOU-ALL. Aliens are living Unthinkable Ages, and often Envy our Mortality. So, they're Double-Crossing Leaders of Nations, into Combative WAR-FAIRS (WARFARE).

REBELLION =REBEL-LION @ the OFFICE is OFF-ICE for Toiling Competitions which aren't Cool folks. So, we can Protest Injustice for another 5,000 years, but the Bullseye is Micro-deception, and all Oppressions are surrounded by this CON, for Live Entertainment.

MER (PYRAMID) =REM (RAPID EYE MOVEMENT). It is also short for MURDER and Programmed folks for Chaos. So, JUSTICE IS JUST-ICE, and they're Plenty of Weapons that aren't designed to Protect Citizens, because the Bandits are mostly Authorities for Cash.

CRUSH =SEE-RUSH in Kindling of Strife, Plundering of Cities, and Murder occur often, because these are Extraterrestrials having TUBE REAL LIFE LIVE FUN! So, don't throw that Brick at Folks, Beat your Fellow People, Light Fires, and Squeeze the Trigger on Guns.

VIRUS =VIRE-US, and PLAGUED means PLAY-GUIDE Diseases can also be turned ON OR OFF, by utilizing EC Metals, to CORE-ON-A-VIRUS (CORONAVIRUS).

Aliens are Enraptured by Death from Disease, which seems to be their #1 Entertainment Live. Pandemics started recurring, During Neolithic Times, and this Wrath is done like Changeovers for Fortifying Ethnic Trends, by also causing Prejudice WAR-RANTS daily.

"-GOD TOLD ME TO DO IT."

Why Dehumanization Persist today? If our real World Leaders, that Stay out of the Limelight, could tell Citizens why they're Harming them? They will likely Articulate what Ancient Priest, frequently, said for over 3 Millenniums, after Killing 1000s of Men, Women, and Children in just a single day, "**GOD TOLD ME TO DO IT.**"

Serial Rapist and Pedophiles are often Saying "**GOD TOLD ME TO DO IT**" too! So, this Evil Reigns, in our Livelihoods, by Extraterrestrials Micro-deception. So, it's Critical not to Disdain Human Beings who are MORE-ON from Alien Demons, that Stages and Cause Harm to others.

"-GOD TOLD ME TO DO IT."

Temple Commandment Codes can come in a Vortex, just like an App Downloading, which Affect Dopamine and Temptations. Gods tell us things not to do, and we try this anyway. But Acting Unruly, Breaking the Law, Being a Gangster, Drinking Alcohol, Using Drugs, Multiple Sexual Desires, Gambling, Warring, and Desecrating Rival Gods, are often what they Program Humankind to do, by Insisting Amoral Scripts, for Enduring Alien Pleasures.

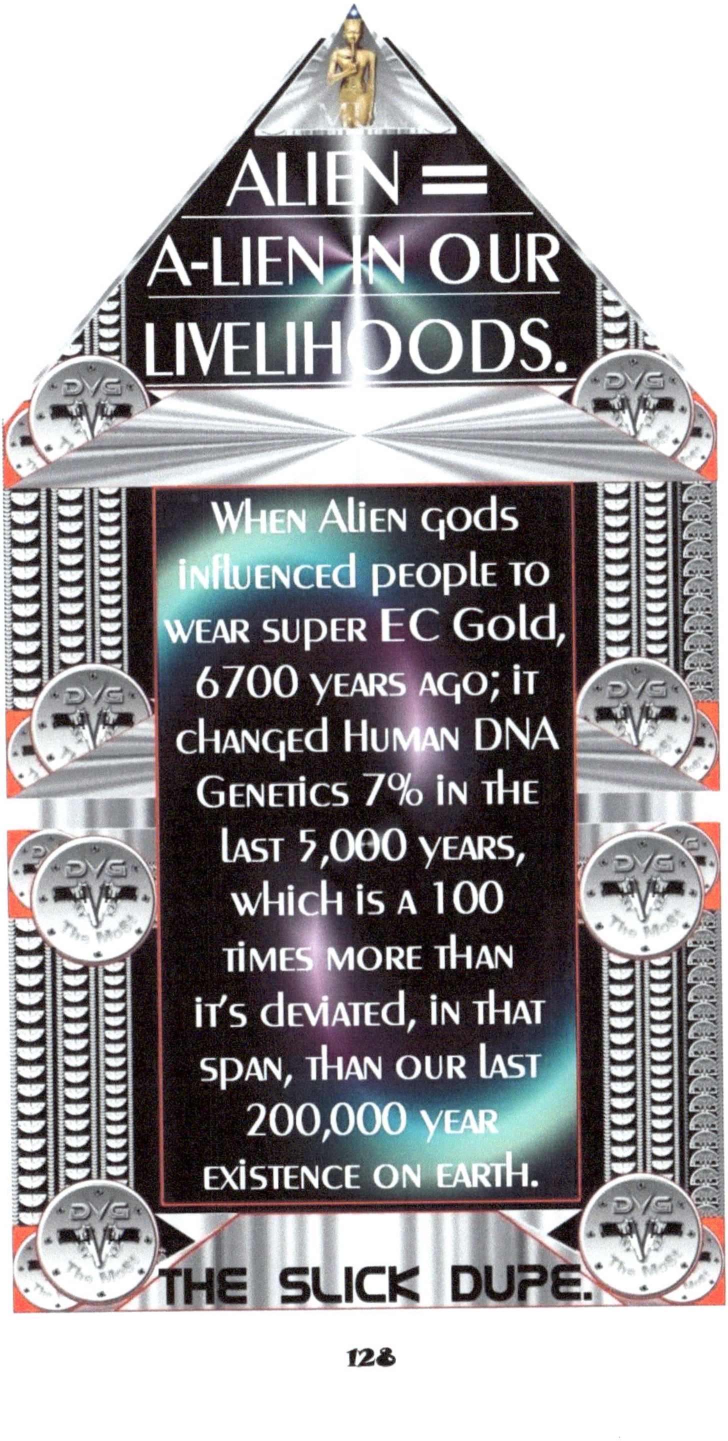
ALIEN =
A-LIEN IN OUR
LIVELIHOODS.
DVG
The Most
When Alien gods influenced people to wear super EC Gold, 6700 years ago; it changed Human DNA Genetics 7% in the last 5,000 years, which is a 100 times more than it's deviated, in that span, than our last 200,000 year existence on earth.
THE SLICK DUPE.

DAMN =DAM-INSIDE US! WE ALL HAVE A-DAM (ADAM) LIEN TO DISPLAY 24 HOUR LIVE SCRIPTS, CONSPIRED BY HIDDEN EVIL BEINGS WHO HAVE ACHIEVED THE MOST TODAY. POSSIBLY, PEOPLE WON'T RIVAL THESE OPPRESSIONS BECAUSE OF VICTORIOUS POWER ALIEN'S HAVE NOW GAINED FROM CLEVER CONTROL ELEMENTS AND NEWER TEMPT STONE STRUCTURES. SO, HUMANS MUST STAND TODAY, AND ABOLISH THIS GLOBAL CON.

NEWER =NEW-ER, AND WE'RE PRODUCING DOLT INVENTIONS, FOR UNSEEMLY LUXURY, WHICH BENEFIT EXTRATERRESTRIALS DAILY. LIKE DRUGS, VACCINES, FACTORIES, ASPHALT ROADS, TEMPT SKYSCRAPERS, FARMER CHEMICAL FERTILIZERS, PROCESSED FOODS, AND WAVELENGTH SIGNAL POLLUTION. PERHAPS, OUR FREE INTELLECTUALS CAN RIVAL ALIENS, AND REPEAL CON GLOBALLY.

Artificial Intelligence (AI) is Newer Dark Forces and we're now exposed to Radiation Pollution for DNA Mutation. So, we're being duped and should disregard all new Technology Research until Humankind Independence is established from Extraterrestrial Deceptions Worldwide.

Quantum Engineering, new Perplex Simulated Worlds, and Longevity should be accomplished soon after. Humankind hasn't experienced real life without Despicable Oppression in a while.

We should never take advice from Rival Beings, and I don't approve of using TUBE Technology to Dehumanize Humans Live; this isn't needed because these Perplex Simulated Pleasures are 100 times Superior, than our Pitiful Lives, itself.

INSIGHT TO WHAT'S RIGHT.

At-last, on May 17th, 2022, the United States of America House Intelligence Committee, had a Meeting to Insight what Humans now call "Unidentified Aerial Phenomena (UAP). "

Recognizing this Alien Technology, is a huge step forward to our Independence by sinister Hidden Forces that's Oppressing Humankind Victorious, for Live Entertainment, every day.

Human Ancestors noted UAP Similar Objects for 1000s of years. But this was Hindered by the Widespread use of Monotheism, which is nothing other than over 4,000 New Religion Applications (Apps), for Alien Entertainment.

Perhaps, May 17, will be remembered as the day Humanity, "Insight To What's Right" and thought outside this Sinister BOX (BE-OXEN).

Today, 10-12% of the World's Population, live in the Southern Hemisphere. But this Air is Superior to the Earths Northern Hemisphere.

Moreover, this is because our Planet Oceans, surrounding these Lands, have lesser Gas and Diesel Transports Polluting our Troposphere.

INSIGHT TO WHAT'S RIGHT.

Humanity should often live near the Equator, like most Great Apes, because it accumulates more Sun UV, for Vitamin D; the Weather is also more Superior and Stable in this Region.

The Enemy also knows this, which is why the Equator is 10 times more Polluted by Broken Engine Transports, being dumped into these Developing Countries, with missing Catalytic Convertors spewing Blacker Smoke each day.

Sadly, it seems, no-one knows these Vehicles are designed to deprive Humans Health daily. And most Drive with all their Windows down!

A Functional Gasoline Car Engine could Kill a Man, in Minutes, by closing the Garage Door while it's running. Noteworthy, a Car stuck in Traffic with Black or Blue Smoke spewing the Air, is like sitting very close to a Building Fire!

CLEAN =SEE-LEAN. True Beings will seek this first and wouldn't Pollute their Environment. I once made Gasoline Engines on Assembly Lines, but was sad that we Built Death Traps, when the Free Thinkers Hydrogen Transports will Excel Health and Wane Global Warming.

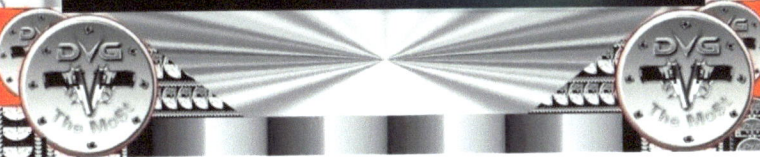

INSIGHT TO WHAT'S RIGHT.

CRASH =SEE-RASH, and people should avoid all Crash Topics concerning RACE (OUR-ACE), because we're making Shows, for our Central Enemy, who control Human Beings Fate now.

Misinformed folks also Blame Themselves for their Unruly Behavior. But we're Hindered by Demolition Programs to Kill the Truth! So, it's not our fault, and Superior Horizons are near.

Continuously, for over 5,000 Dreadful Years, Humans had a Quest, to BE-LESS (BLESS), for a Bait called CASH, which indicates SEE-ASH.

Are you A-WAKE (AWAKE)? I hope Humanity Answer is No! Sadly, People are Prostituting, Acting Buffoonery, Killing their Oppositions, and now getting more Sinister Views Online, by Misusing Crash Topics, for making Money.

PLAY =PEE-LAY, and this is what occurs when folks put on a CONDOM and have Sex with a Stranger; this is why it mean SEE-ON-DUMB.

Homophones and Anadromes are Roots of all Words made to be Amusing for Alien Gods, & not a WHO-MAN-BEING (HUMAN BEING).

INSIGHT TO WHAT'S RIGHT.

Since Ancient Times, Human Beings liked to Dance and Mingle at Nightclubs? Although, it was called this, because you'd often see a NIGHT-CLUB, upside your Head, from Drunk and Unruly People seeking a PEE-LAY (PLAY).

CLASH =SEE-LASH. It is time for Humankind to "Insight To What's Right" now, to Prevent the Mighty Enemy LASH from often Striking Humans, on the Earth daily, Ladies and Gents.

I-DO-STAND, and will never UNDER-STAND to CON. So, get off your Knees Humankind; these are the Enemy Programs, Implemented to Control People's Fate, like Computer Apps.

AMEN =A-ME-INSIDE, and we should realize that we're living in a clever PLAY-NETWORK (PLANET) Designed for Rival Beings Pleasure.

It seems Alien UAP Spheres, can also protect the Earth from Building Size Asteroids, which can obliterate many Big Cities in seconds, to Perpetuate their Victorious PLAY-NETWORK.

The Enemy biggest CON is the afterlife folks, which are Simulated Worlds, that Humanity could Experience by using TUBE Technologies.

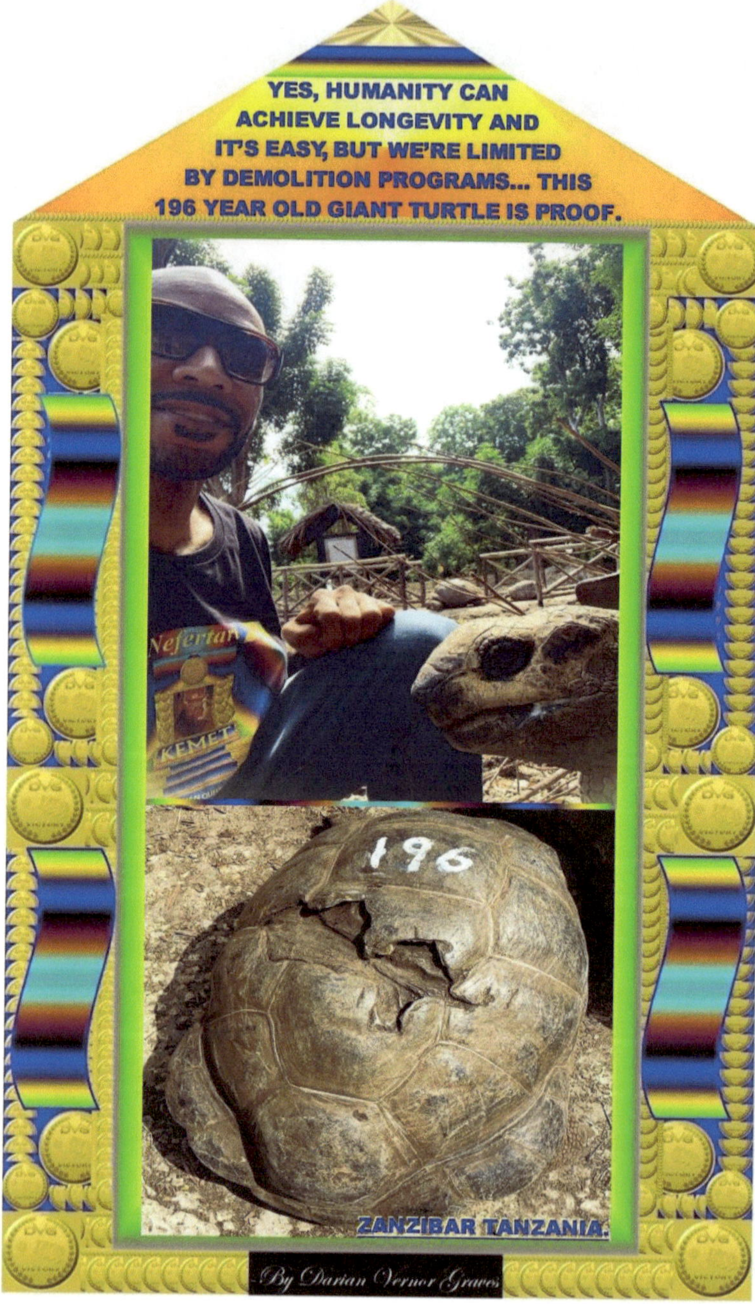
YES, HUMANITY CAN
ACHIEVE LONGEVITY AND
IT'S EASY, BUT WE'RE LIMITED
BY DEMOLITION PROGRAMS... THIS
196 YEAR OLD GIANT TURTLE IS PROOF.
KEMET
196
ZANZIBAR TANZANIA.
By Darian Vernor Graves

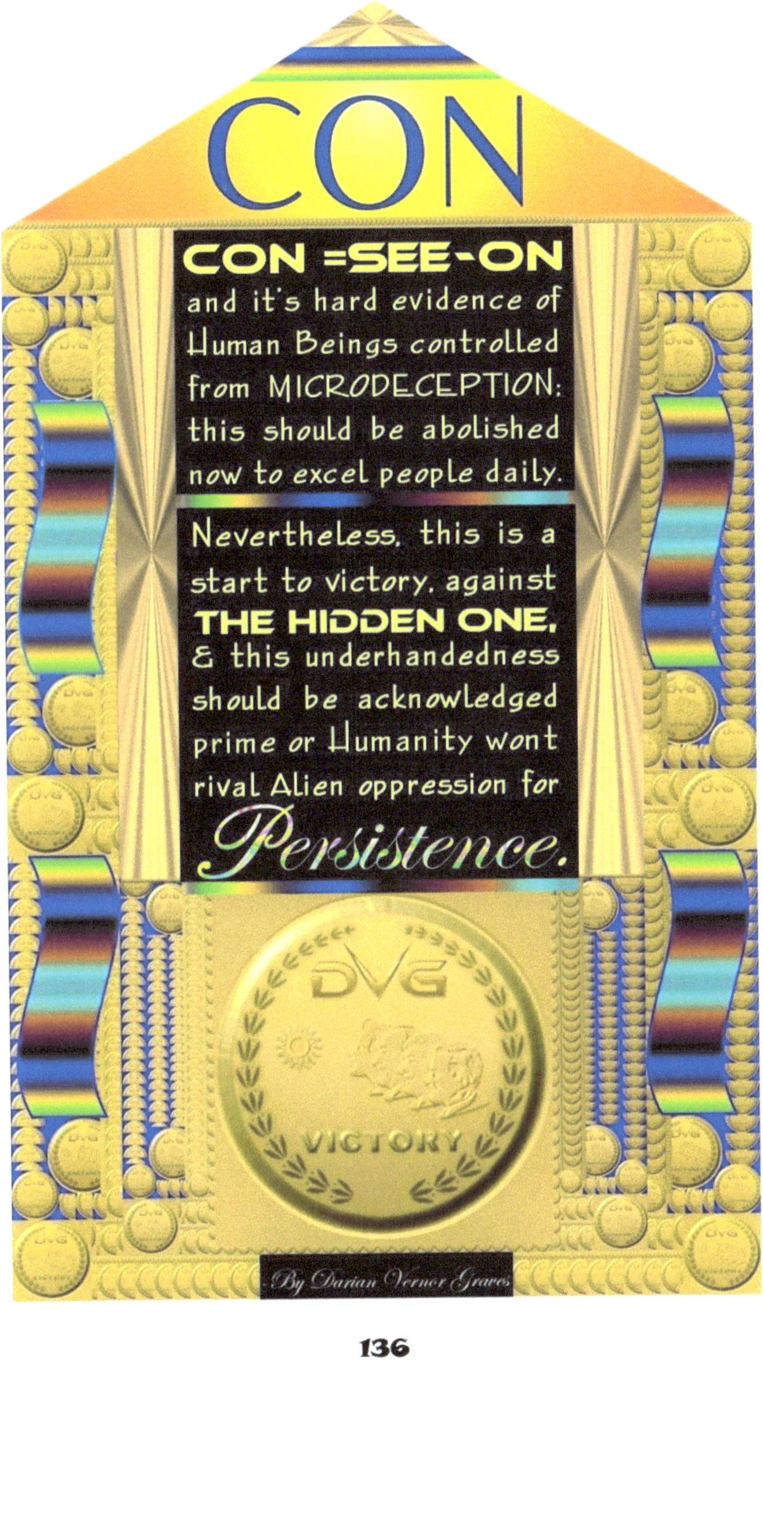

CON
CON =SEE-ON
and it's hard evidence of
Human Beings controlled
from MICRODECEPTION:
this should be abolished
now to excel people daily.
Nevertheless, this is a
start to victory, against
THE HIDDEN ONE,
& this underhandedness
should be acknowledged
prime or Humanity wont
rival Alien oppression for
Persistence.
DVG
VICTORY
By Darian Vernor Graves

THE AFRICAN TRUTH.

KEMET

PAWN =PAW-INSIDE, because it's a clever DOG (GOD) inside people now, and we Demolition Ourselves for Profits today. So, don't TEACH-ER (TEACHER), to Human Beings, Ladies and Gents.

GENOME =GENOCIDE-ME. Therefore, Humanity isn't Progressing in Childbirths, from Evolution Adaptations, which Mammals utilize to Prosper.

Around several decades ago, Scientists proved Melanated Afro Africans have a Genome, which Developed from Ultraviolet Light by our Sun, near Earths Equator, that gave them Superior Abilities in Health, Endurance, and Intelligence.

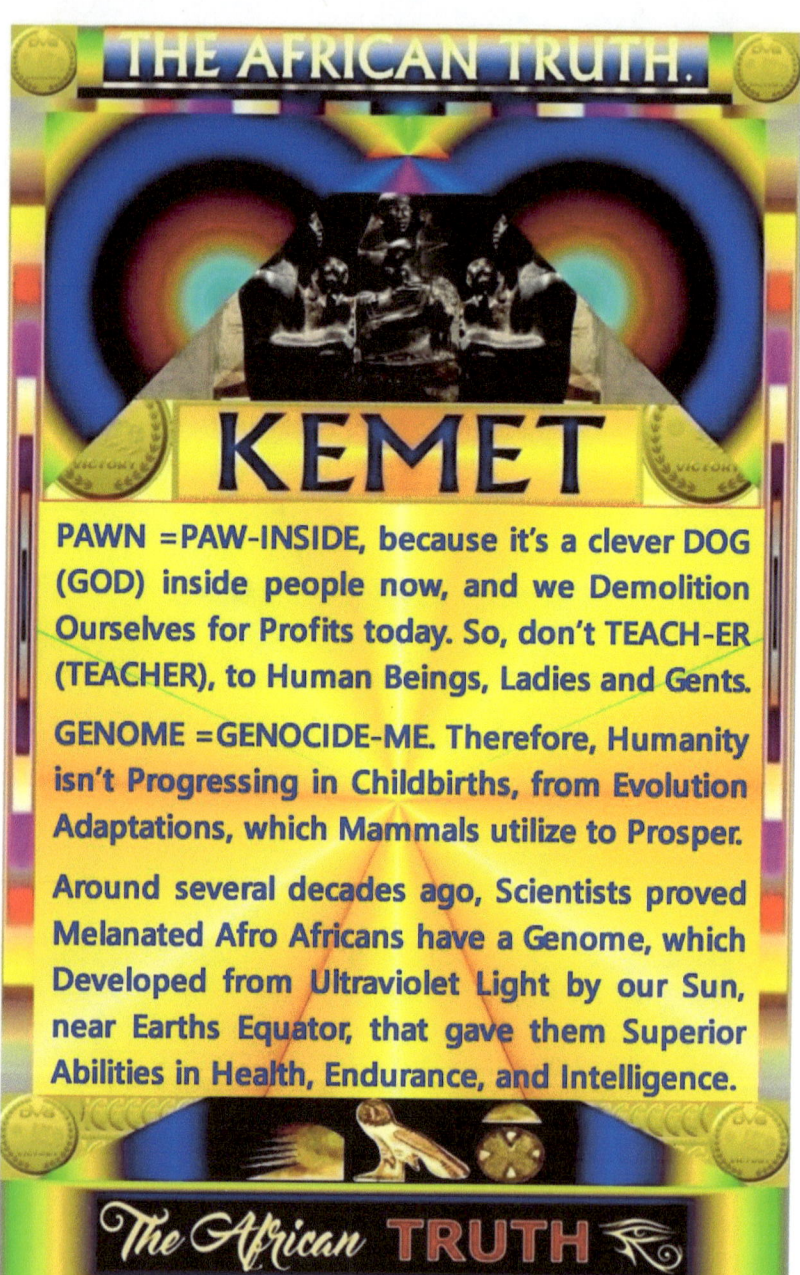

The African TRUTH

THE AFRICAN TRUTH.

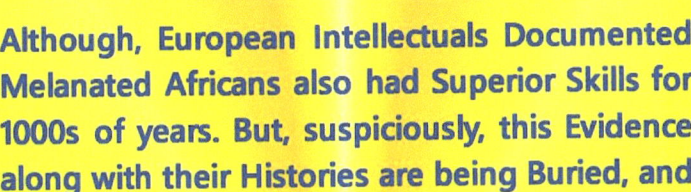

Although, European Intellectuals Documented Melanated Africans also had Superior Skills for 1000s of years. But, suspiciously, this Evidence along with their Histories are being Buried, and who changed the way they're Portrayed today?

Further vexing is after Verifying this Truth. So, why aren't Light Skin People taking advantage of having Greater Abilities for their Children to fight off Diseases, Run like the Wind, and have Greater Odds of Performing Superior as Pupils?

Alien God's Devised this, and want all Babies to Grow into A-DOLT (ADULT)! The CON is African Humans are Lesser Superb. So, it's Easier to be Light Toned, with Stringy Hair, and Tougher to have Melanated Skin, with Afro Curly Hair, now.

Consequently, BLACK means BE-LACK, NEGRO signifies KNEE-GROW, and Melanated Africans Largest Language Speaking Category, Termed BANTU, indicates BE-ANT-YOU, for Discrediting their Higher-Ranking Existence for Humankind.

The African TRUTH

THE AFRICAN TRUTH.

Note, once Humankind Achieve Longevity and TUBE Technologies? How we Look will become Obsolete, but the Alien God's PLAY-NETWORK is Victorious and Hindering us from attaining it.

Melanated Skin is Prime, but it's a Pry to Aliens Pale People Experiences now. So, Godforsaken Prejudice, routinely, Prevent it from Prospering.

Case, when a Powerful Light-Toned Skin Person, with Stringy Hair, Shakes a Common Melanated Humans Hand in Public? They are often being Ridiculed from their Peers and the Masses now.

Humanities Master Spring is also Afro-Hair, and it's an Ultimate Status which Simplified Human Options when Choosing Suitors with Prominent Abilities; it's just like Elephants Preferring Male Mates, with Bigger Tusks, for Surviving Wildlife.

Afro-Hair is also more Superior because it isn't Hollow and doesn't Store Head Louse Eggs; this is a Pest Matter for those with Stringy Hair, like Apes, which often needs Grooming from others.

The African TRUTH

THE AFRICAN TRUTH.

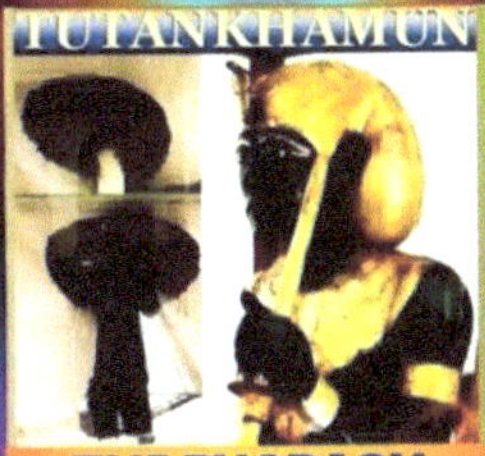

THE PHARAOH TUTANKHAMUN WORE THIS AFRO-WIG WITH PRIDE & DIGNITY IN 1323 BCE.

The African TRUTH

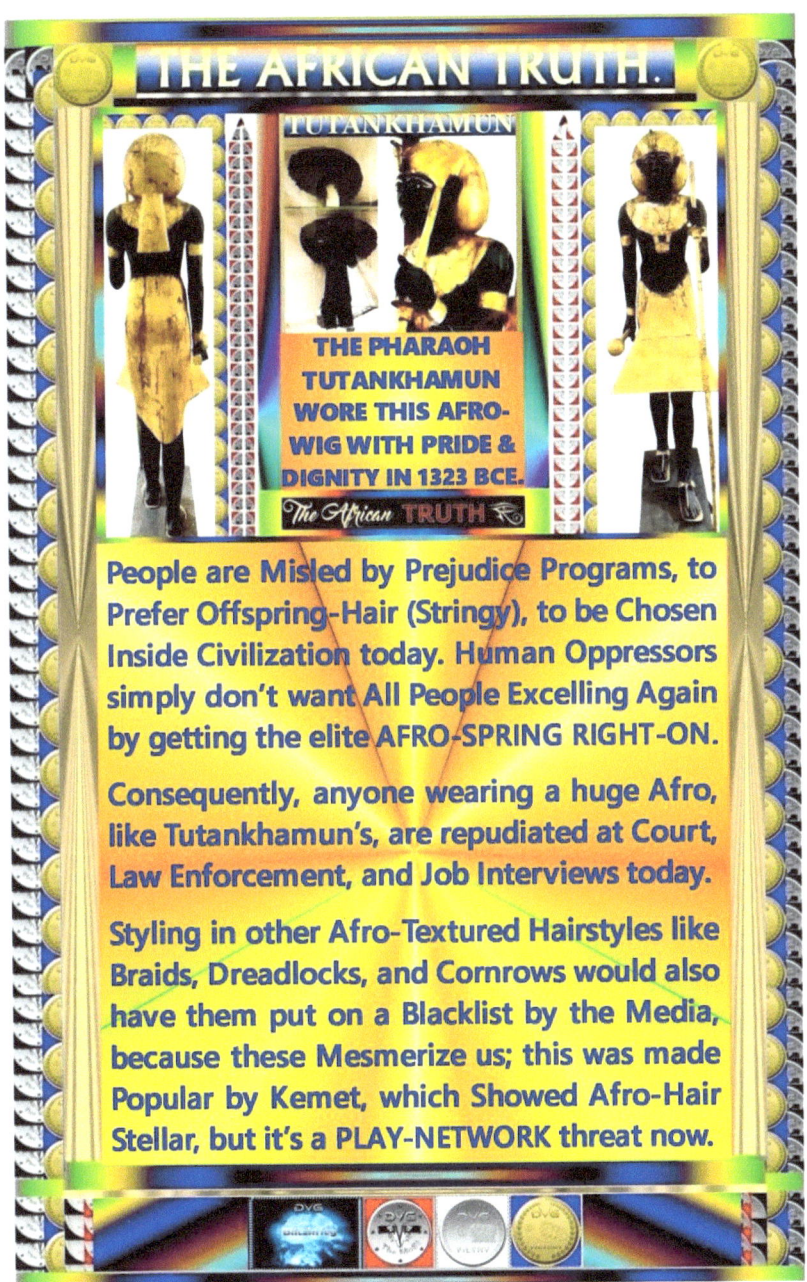

People are Misled by Prejudice Programs, to Prefer Offspring-Hair (Stringy), to be Chosen Inside Civilization today. Human Oppressors simply don't want All People Excelling Again by getting the elite AFRO-SPRING RIGHT-ON.

Consequently, anyone wearing a huge Afro, like Tutankhamun's, are repudiated at Court, Law Enforcement, and Job Interviews today.

Styling in other Afro-Textured Hairstyles like Braids, Dreadlocks, and Cornrows would also have them put on a Blacklist by the Media, because these Mesmerize us; this was made Popular by Kemet, which Showed Afro-Hair Stellar, but it's a PLAY-NETWORK threat now.

THE AFRICAN TRUTH.
AFRICAN ART GALLERY
QUEEN TIYE
ARUSHA TANZANIA

BLACKLIST =BE-LACK-LIST. Kemetic Melanated History, and their African names, that are still being used by Tribes, are being suppressed now.

Unfortunately, I lived at 8 Countries in Africa, for years. But only met just one-person outside Egypt, that knew what Kemet was, and it was an, exemplary, Woman Living Inside Botswana.

This is recurring because Schools and Museums Worldwide are Hindering Melanated folks from Learning they Created the first Civilizations, on Africa's Nile River, to Decline their Intelligence.

Arusha's African Art Gallery Museum has Awful Statue Scenes of Slaves and how they view Afro Africans. But I didn't see Melanated Artwork of Kings, Queens, and Genius like Imhotep known to Inspire our Youth into Better Horizons today.

But the Transgressions from Slavery, Jim Crow Laws, and Apartheid are Accepted; this is often Schemed to Deter Light-Toned People not to be Superior Afro Africans, and it deceive folks into thinking they Erected Advanced Giza Pyramids.

BRILLIANT =BE-OUR-ILL-EYE-ANT, but Humans in Power believe taking away African History is utilized for controlling these people Minds, like USA Slavery Times, to Pay them cheaper wages now? But it's CLEVERER than that Dolt Agenda.

By Darian Vernor Graves

CLEVERER =SEE-LEVER-ER. Afro Africans, that lives near the Equator, have the easiest path to Longevity. So, there's added Demolition Stock, led by Broke Engine Transports, Foods, and HIV Diseases Aimed to Weak their Immune System.

The Most Disgraceful Things, I Saw, During My Numerous Travels at Africa's Equator; were the amount of Black and Blue Smoke Spewing from Broke Transports daily. But it doesn't end there.

I was more surprised, when learning the people were paying over 10 times more for these older Vehicles! Broke Engine Cars are mostly crushed and sold for Scrap Metals inside the USA today.

Although, I did research, before flying. But this Broken Engine Smoke Pollution is very Bad, and much Higher than what's often Relisted Online.

Sadly, I met no-one complaining, because Cash Profits were High, and these Vehicles doubled, on Numerous African Roads, in the last 8 years.

Worse, Cities near the Equator have 100 times more Stark Motorcycles, on African Roadways, with Bad Engines Spewing Crazy Hydrocarbons.

Therefore, I had to Wear 2 Mask, when Driving in Traffic, or Sense Nose-Pain and Headaches. Too many people were also Killed in Accidents!

By Darian Vernor Graves

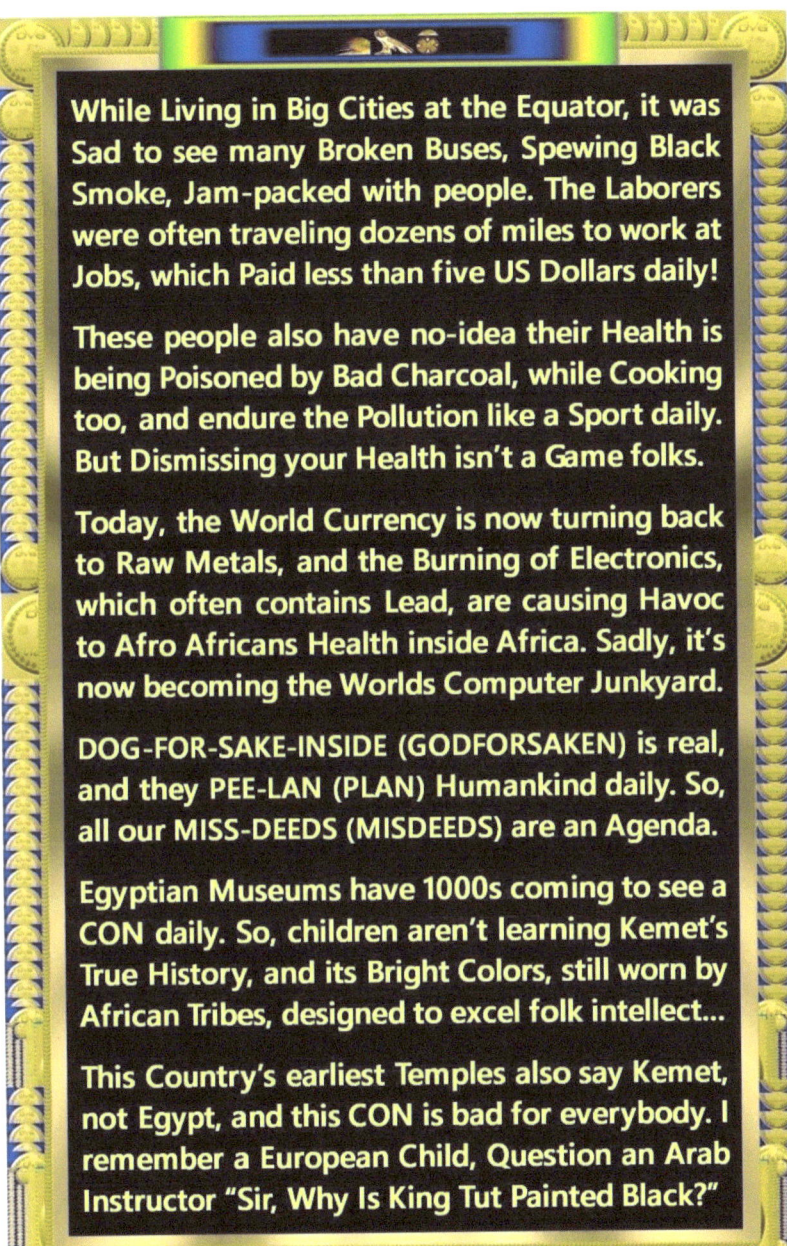

While Living in Big Cities at the Equator, it was Sad to see many Broken Buses, Spewing Black Smoke, Jam-packed with people. The Laborers were often traveling dozens of miles to work at Jobs, which Paid less than five US Dollars daily!

These people also have no-idea their Health is being Poisoned by Bad Charcoal, while Cooking too, and endure the Pollution like a Sport daily. But Dismissing your Health isn't a Game folks.

Today, the World Currency is now turning back to Raw Metals, and the Burning of Electronics, which often contains Lead, are causing Havoc to Afro Africans Health inside Africa. Sadly, it's now becoming the Worlds Computer Junkyard.

DOG-FOR-SAKE-INSIDE (GODFORSAKEN) is real, and they PEE-LAN (PLAN) Humankind daily. So, all our MISS-DEEDS (MISDEEDS) are an Agenda.

Egyptian Museums have 1000s coming to see a CON daily. So, children aren't learning Kemet's True History, and its Bright Colors, still worn by African Tribes, designed to excel folk intellect...

This Country's earliest Temples also say Kemet, not Egypt, and this CON is bad for everybody. I remember a European Child, Question an Arab Instructor "Sir, Why Is King Tut Painted Black?"

By Darian Vernor Graves

THE AFRICAN TRUTH.

KING TUT & KING MENTUHOTEP II

CAIRO MUSEUM SAID THIS TO A CHILD.

"Oh, when the Pharaoh's died, they wanted to become a black god of the underworld Osiris?"

But God Osiris is always painted green folks. Ancient Kemet Mummies Hue, like Pharaoh Thutmoses IV and Merneptah shown above, are clear evidence that Afro Africans started this Civilization; I explain and display more in my book called Kemet, The African Truth.

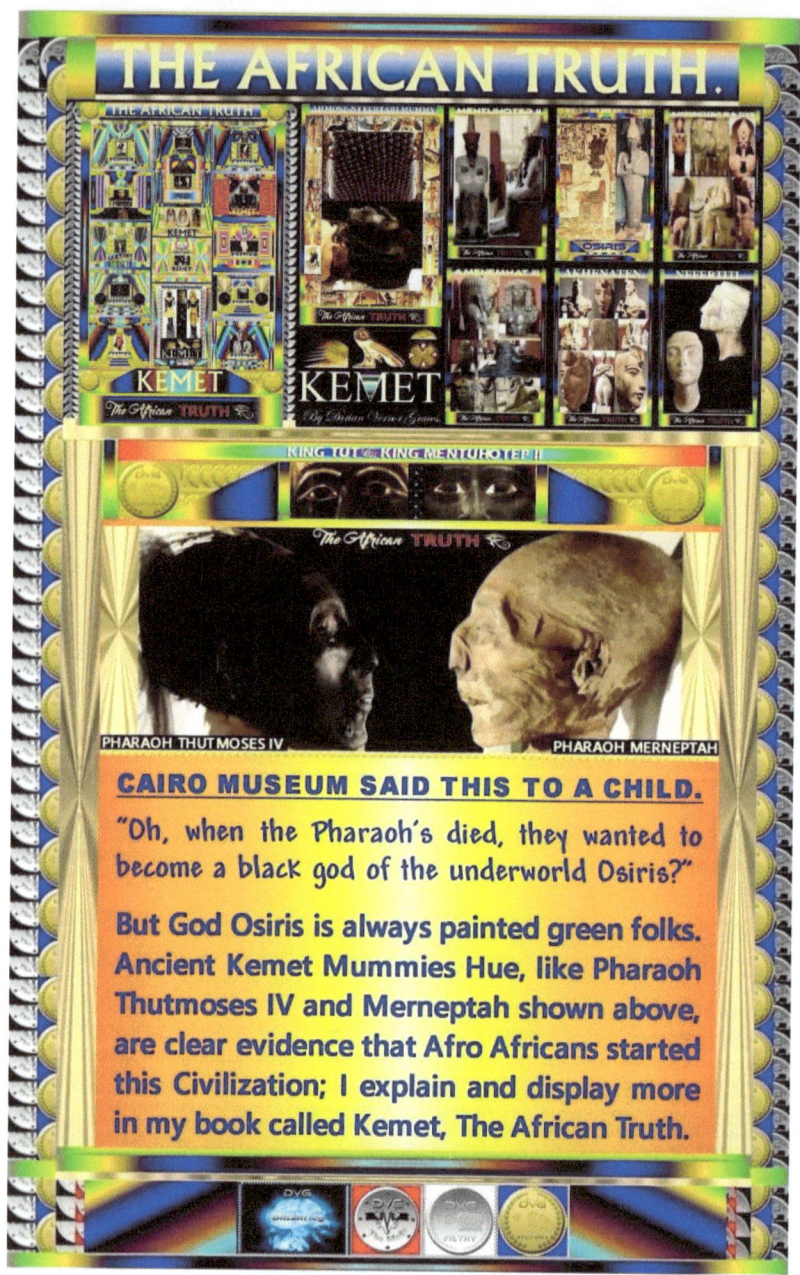

THE AFRICAN TRUTH.

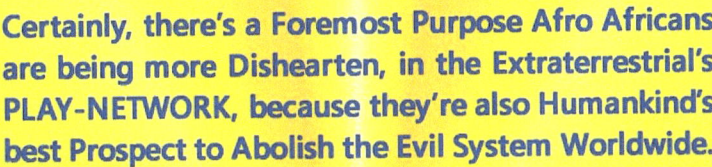

Certainly, there's a Foremost Purpose Afro Africans are being more Dishearten, in the Extraterrestrial's PLAY-NETWORK, because they're also Humankind's best Prospect to Abolish the Evil System Worldwide.

Furthermore, this also last happened from Pharaoh Tutankhamun's Stellar Father Akhenaten and Queen Nefertiti, about 3,350 years ago, in Ancient Kemet.

Beware of the PEE-REACH-ER (PREACHER)! To have Superior Control of Afro Africans. Alien God's Priest Insisted all the Pharaohs to Marry their Half-Sisters.

Incest Diseases caused Havoc to Humans Offspring Health, like Epilepsy and Congenital Disorders; this also created more Ethnics for Alien's Entertainment.

It seems Pharaoh Akhenaten was able to rival clever Alien God's, during this time, because of the Crucial Decision from his Father Amenhotep III; this Man Married Tiye and not a Sister, cited by Kemet Priest.

Note, what Akhenaten Accomplished was Elite in all History; this Man was Definitely Thinking Clear, and Saw the CON of these Alien God's. So, he Abolished all of them rapidly, and Worshiped the ATEN (SUN).

The African TRUTH

THE AFRICAN TRUTH.

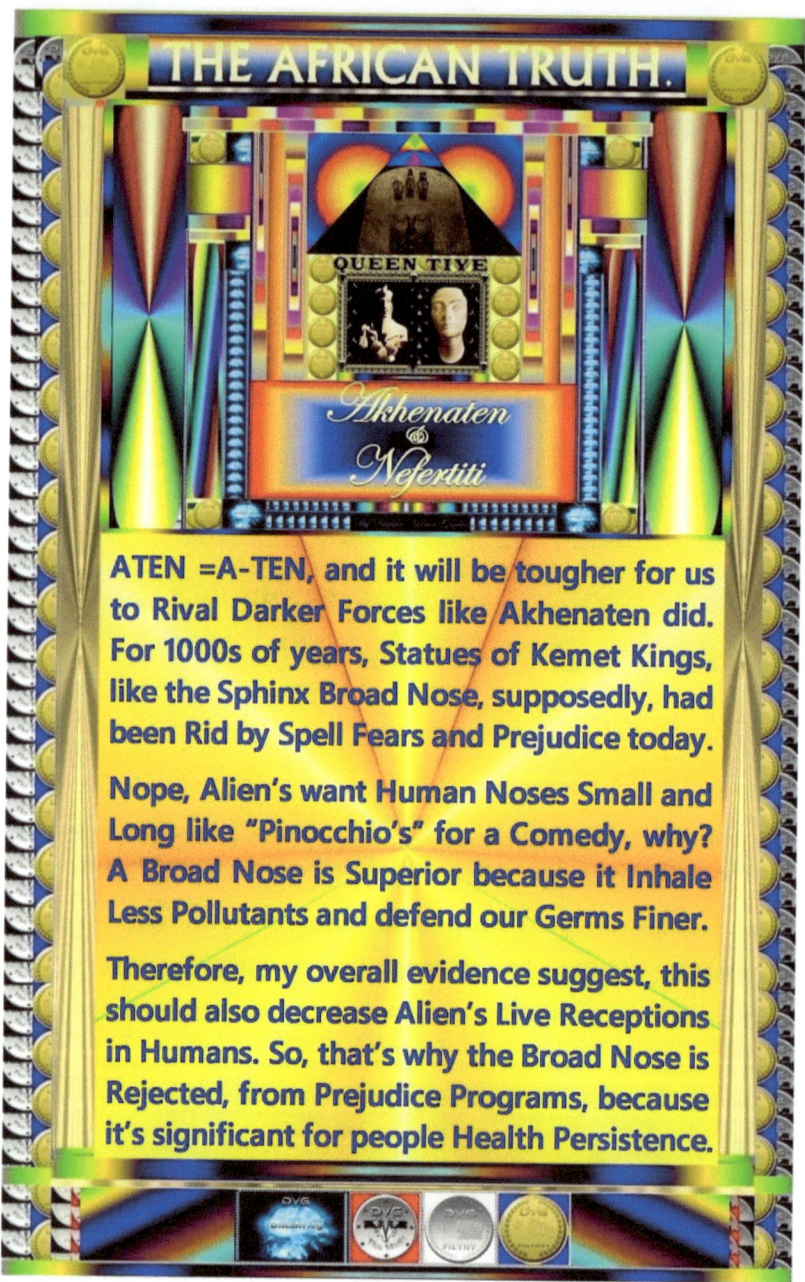

ATEN =A-TEN, and it will be tougher for us to Rival Darker Forces like Akhenaten did. For 1000s of years, Statues of Kemet Kings, like the Sphinx Broad Nose, supposedly, had been Rid by Spell Fears and Prejudice today.

Nope, Alien's want Human Noses Small and Long like "Pinocchio's" for a Comedy, why? A Broad Nose is Superior because it Inhale Less Pollutants and defend our Germs Finer.

Therefore, my overall evidence suggest, this should also decrease Alien's Live Receptions in Humans. So, that's why the Broad Nose is Rejected, from Prejudice Programs, because it's significant for people Health Persistence.

Women are also a threat in this PLAY-NETWORK. So, they've been more oppressed in the last 5,500 years. Likely, because they're Extra Multi-Tasked, Living Longer than Men, and are saying No, to Evil recurring, better than Males stand for Humankind.

For these reasons, it seems Women are targeted to consume more Demolition Products, that deprives Health, to weaken their Superior Abilities on Earth.

Women are lured to Toxic Chemicals in Cosmetics, Lotions, Hair Goods, and Bad Birth Control Pills; they're also getting their Nail-Polish done, inside High-Risk Salons, with a Flurry of Dangers in Paint.

Not all African Genetics are the same, and before the Nilo-Saharans ventured to a Lush Sahara; it seems they also came from the PLAY-NETWORK #1 Source Catalholyuk, in Turkey, which bred new Races and bizarre rituals that spread around Earth.

Nilo is shorter for "Nile." The Stellar Nilo-Saharans still mostly live inside Sudan and has the Darkest Melanated Skin today; they also launched the first known Civilization, on Africa's Nile River in Ta-Seti (Sudan), which eventually spread to Kemet (Egypt).

The Bantu speaking peoples, in Africa, are mostly, descendants of Nilo-Saharans, and they adopted similar Rituals, which are still utilized widely today.

AFRICA

EAST AFRICA STILL HAS THE BEST YEAR AROUND WEATHER IN THE WORLD. THIS IS ALSO WHY MANY OF THE OLDEST MODERN HUMAN BEING BONES WERE FOUND THERE.

KEMET PEOPLE KNEW THIS TOO. SO, MANY TRAVELED THERE FOR ITS COOLER SUMMERS & RARE WHITE BEACHES.

PHARAOH HATSHEPSUT CONSTRUCTED A TEMPLE COMMEMORATED FOR HER EXPEDITIONS TO PUNT (SOMALIA). THIS WOMAN ALSO UPGRADED THE STATUS OF WOMEN DURING HER OVER 20 YEAR REIGN IN KEMET.

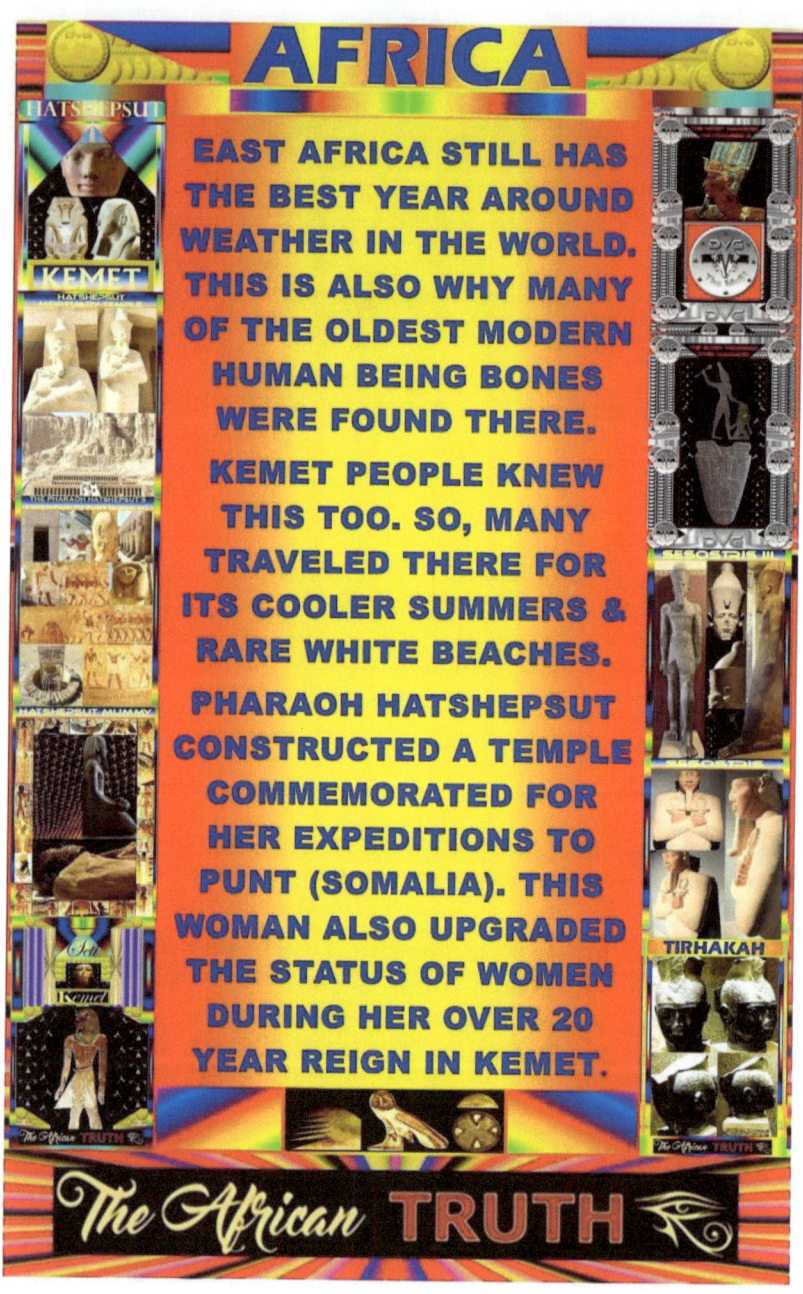

The African TRUTH

AFRICA

TODAY, JUST LIKE THE KEMET TIMES, PEOPLE CHOOSE TO LIVE IN HOTTER DESERTS AND FRIGID WEATHER YEARLY, BECAUSE OF PRIDE OR BETTER JOBS.

AFRICA IS ALSO BEING BLACKLISTED BECAUSE OF PREJUDICE. SO, RICH PEOPLE ARE RARELY INVESTING IN NEW DEVELOPMENT THERE TO DEPRIVE AFRICANS.

SADLY, THIS IS WHAT THE ENEMY WANT MOST HUMANS TO DO. SO, IT'S WEIRD TO SEE LACKING CONTINENTS THRIVING AND THE BEST LAND ON THE PLANET ISN'T NOW.

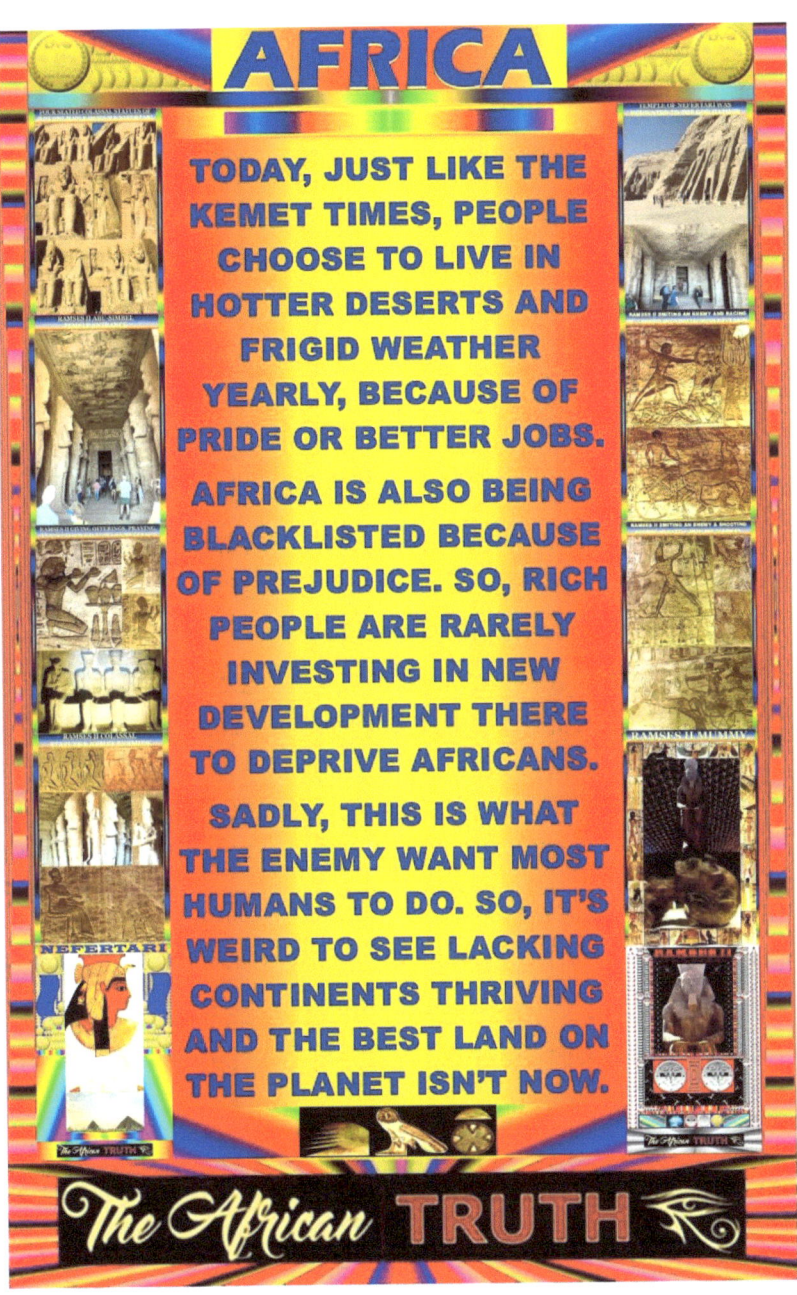

The African TRUTH

BRIGHTEST =BE-RIGHT-ESTABLISHED, and Humans Brightest, I've encountered on Earth, are these San people inside Botswana; it was great to talk to self-sufficient folks who knows all the Evil of Civilization and doesn't want a LEADER, which means LEAD-ER.

BUILDING =BE-YOU-ILL-DING. The San doesn't like Mainstream people doing the same Toiling things, on their Job every day, like an oxen going in circles.

The San also disapprove living inside Public Houses because they're like Prisons, that the Nomadic San, remarkably, Recognized are Depriving Folks Health.

The San disdained doing Art Paintings because they noticed Chemicals in this Paint were Poisoning their Health. And Smelting Heavy Metals, like Gold from Rocks, are Insane things for folks to do at any Price.

The Stellar San have Great Insights that all folks can benefit from and really impressed me; they're also concerned about their Youth, increasingly adopting numerous mainstream bad customs for Cash today.

It seems the San is free of Demolition Programs in the clever PLAY-NETWORK (PLANET). However, the San also says this is fading rapidly, by Government Modernization, and they're no-longer allowed to be free on lands they resided on for over 60,000 years.

Humans are like Dogs and need others to take care for them or Die. But the San just want their Kalahari Lands, to insight being self-sufficient like all should.

GRID is short for GRIDLOCK. Today, nobody should live in the freezing cold and depend on Mainstream Fossil Fuels to survive. So, we should become self-sufficient by getting off this Grid and produce clean Energy from our Sun or Earth's Magnetic Fields now.

BILLIONAIRE =BE-ILL-EYE-ON-AIR, and this is what they did, to the Environment, and became Wealthy since ancient times. Sadly, Demolition Goods are on the Shelves and Most Human Being Foods are made for them to BE-WRECK-FAST (BREAKFAST) for Cash!

Today, people like to Eat CHIPS and SEE-HIPS, but don't research or test all the Dangers of their Foods, like this Dismantling Sugar. Vinegar is also a Sinister Additive, that's Demolishing Humanity Health daily.

Vinegar is in KETCHUP (CATCH-UP), PICKLES (PICK-LESS), and MUSTARD (MUSS-TARD). TARD is short for RETARD and that's what Humans are acting like.

To learn these things, begin with the first Language, Religion, and Foods logged in History today. Test all products and don't take advice from people getting PEE-AID (PAID) to deceive you for SEE-ASH (CASH).

The African TRUTH

Quick Test: Try putting a Chicken Bone in Vinegar and feel how it turns soft, like Noodles, overnight. Also, lay some Concrete inside this Acid, and see it dissolve too!

Are you A-WAKE (AWAKE)? Nope, because you're now recognizing what this Sinister Vinegar must be doing to your Bones, Nerves, and Blood when utilized daily.

Vinegar is a Bad Acid and it's not Natural. So, if you're a Senior or also experiencing Debilitated Health now? Using this will be like making a Clear Pond Foggy, by picking up too much Dirt, or Breaking a Water Dam, that often cause Stroke, Heart Attacks, and Aneurysms.

Beware of the "Special Sauce!" So, when going out to Eat, try ordering Foods Plane, or Flavor it from making fresh Natural Sauce rations, for Optimum Health folks.

Most Humans can't read the Small Printed Labels, on their Water Bottles, which often contains High Levels of terrible Sodium (Salt) and Chloride (Bleach). Note, take Pictures, Zoom in, and Research all the Dangers of these, supposedly, good foods for Optimum Health.

Clean Air is also Essential today. So, taking Carpet out of your Bedrooms, and Moving into one without Rugs are the quickest way, I tested, for debilitated folks to feel better overnight, and that's the Truth Humankind.

Have a Headache now? Try Detoxing, but Computer, Cell Phone, and Internet Radiation are often causing Harm. So, turn off awful WIFI, Personal Hotspot, and utilize Internet Cords or Wire Ear Speakers for Talking.

WATER =WATT-ER, and this is what Mainstream Water has been designed to do, since the Birth of Civilization, 5,500 years ago. Pipes welded with Lead Leach in Water and turns into Batteries in People Body; this cause -ITIS.

You can see Heavy Metals, which turns Water brown, in most Homes; there're no exceptions, when Cooking, and Boiling Water don't subside Lead affects inside Humans.

Be a Chemist, to Control your Health Persistence, from utilizing Distilled Water, for Cooking, and Natural Triple Filtered Spring Water for Drinking. Avoid Bottled Water with Elements mixed inside it, and some contains high Sodium, that are now causing Chronic Health for Profits.

Coconut Water isn't good for those with Lead Toxicity; higher Potassium are inside most Nuts, and this includes Fruits like Bananas, which releases some grim Radiation.

Potassium Rich Foods often causes Harm to folks when combined with Lead. Fruits like Passion, with Abundant Vitamin C, can also make people Sick with Lead Toxicity.

CASHEW =SEE-ASH-EW, and many died too soon with these Volatile Nuts still in their Mouths. Cashew Shells have a Toxin called Urushiol, that Leaches inside the Nut and it can cause Reactions, which include Kidney Stones.

Volcanos are Earth Sewers and often have Toxic Land. So, avoid Living near one or Drinking this Water, which also have Heavy Metals, that does more than stain teeth.

Today, redundant Broke Gasoline Engine Transports, on Developing Country Highways, are releasing Toxic Black Smoke; this is Depriving our Health and causing Disease.

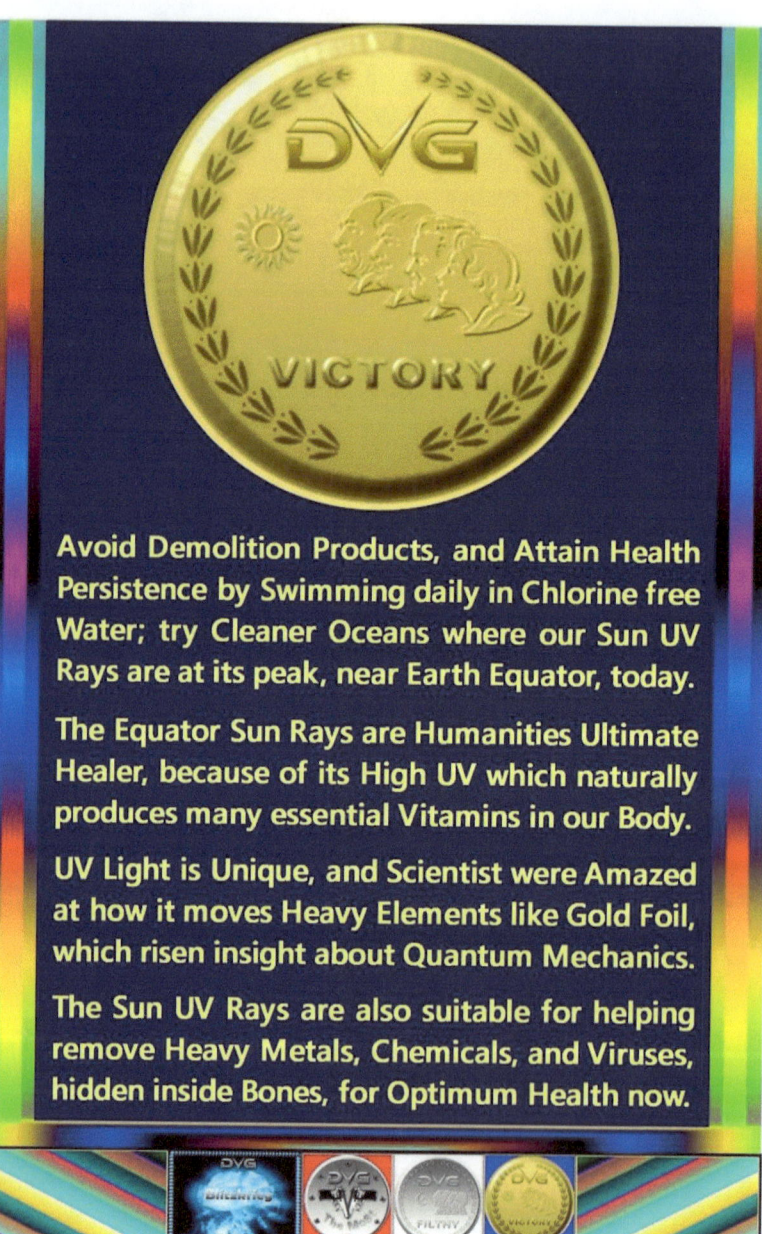

Avoid Demolition Products, and Attain Health Persistence by Swimming daily in Chlorine free Water; try Cleaner Oceans where our Sun UV Rays are at its peak, near Earth Equator, today.

The Equator Sun Rays are Humanities Ultimate Healer, because of its High UV which naturally produces many essential Vitamins in our Body.

UV Light is Unique, and Scientist were Amazed at how it moves Heavy Elements like Gold Foil, which risen insight about Quantum Mechanics.

The Sun UV Rays are also suitable for helping remove Heavy Metals, Chemicals, and Viruses, hidden inside Bones, for Optimum Health now.

God's 24 Hour Play-Network: No-One Can Rival The Most.

HEAVEN =HEAVE-INSIDE, BECAUSE THIS IS A FUN TUBE GAME, FOR ADVANCED BEINGS WHO ALSO ACHIEVED LONGEVITY. PLUS, NO-ONE CAN RIVAL THE MOST REAL LIFE LIVE EXPERIENCE, & ALIENS ARE ENRAPTURED BY OUR 24 HOUR LIVE SHOWS.

TODAY, HUMAN BEINGS ARE DEPLETING WATER AQUIFERS, AND THIS IS A SCHEME FOR AN EPIC GLOBAL DEMISE. HUMANKIND IS BEING SETUP, LIKE THE MINOAN'S (ATLANTIS) MISLED TO ALSO DWELL ON ITS LIVE VOLCANO, TO BROADEN THE EXTRATERRESTRIAL'S PECULIAR GRATIFICATIONS.

BLAME =BE-LAME, AND HUMANS THAT CON ARE BE-OXEN (BOX) TO PROGRAMS. SO, WE SHOULD ABOLISH THE PEE-OW-ER (POWER) NOW BEFORE HUMANKIND CRUMBLE, AND WE'LL SEE-RUMBLE FROM A FLURRY OF NUCLEAR BOMBS, ANY TIME.

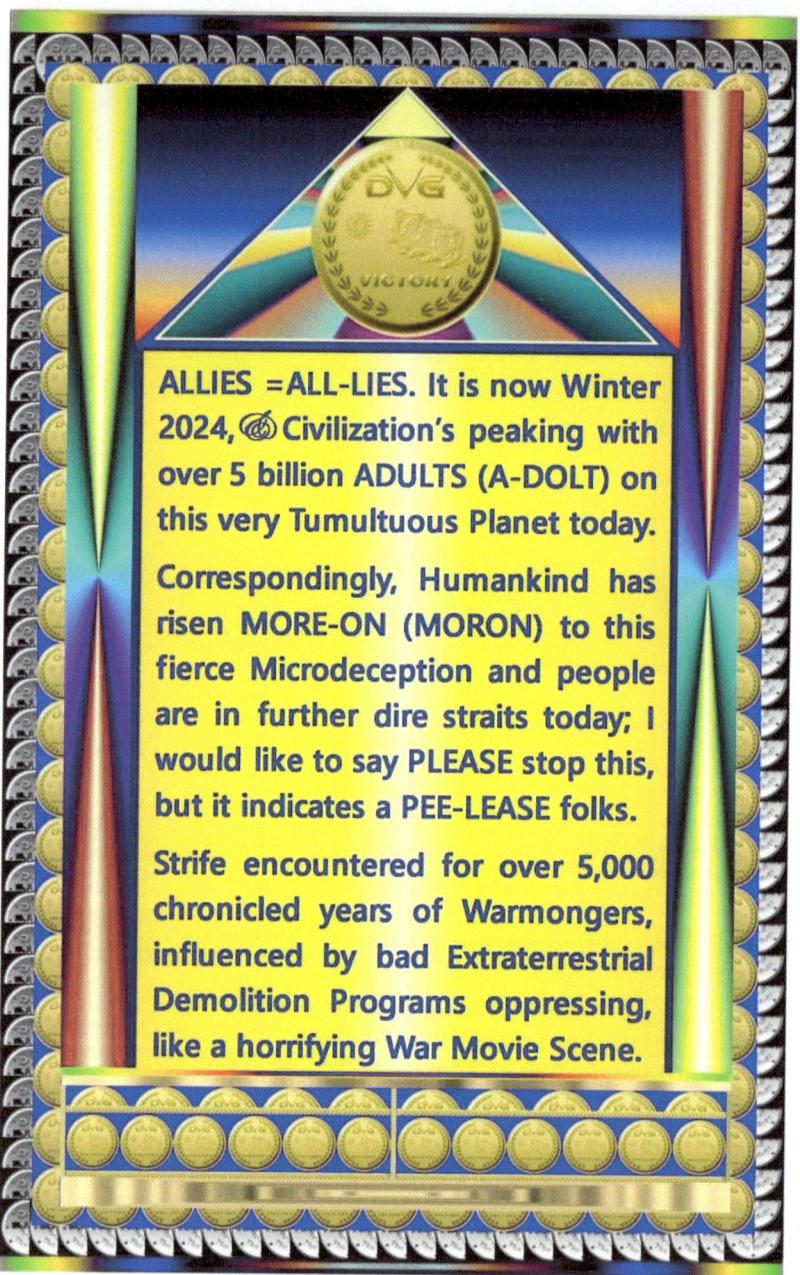

ALLIES =ALL-LIES. It is now Winter 2024, Civilization's peaking with over 5 billion ADULTS (A-DOLT) on this very Tumultuous Planet today.

Correspondingly, Humankind has risen MORE-ON (MORON) to this fierce Microdeception and people are in further dire straits today; I would like to say PLEASE stop this, but it indicates a PEE-LEASE folks.

Strife encountered for over 5,000 chronicled years of Warmongers, influenced by bad Extraterrestrial Demolition Programs oppressing, like a horrifying War Movie Scene.

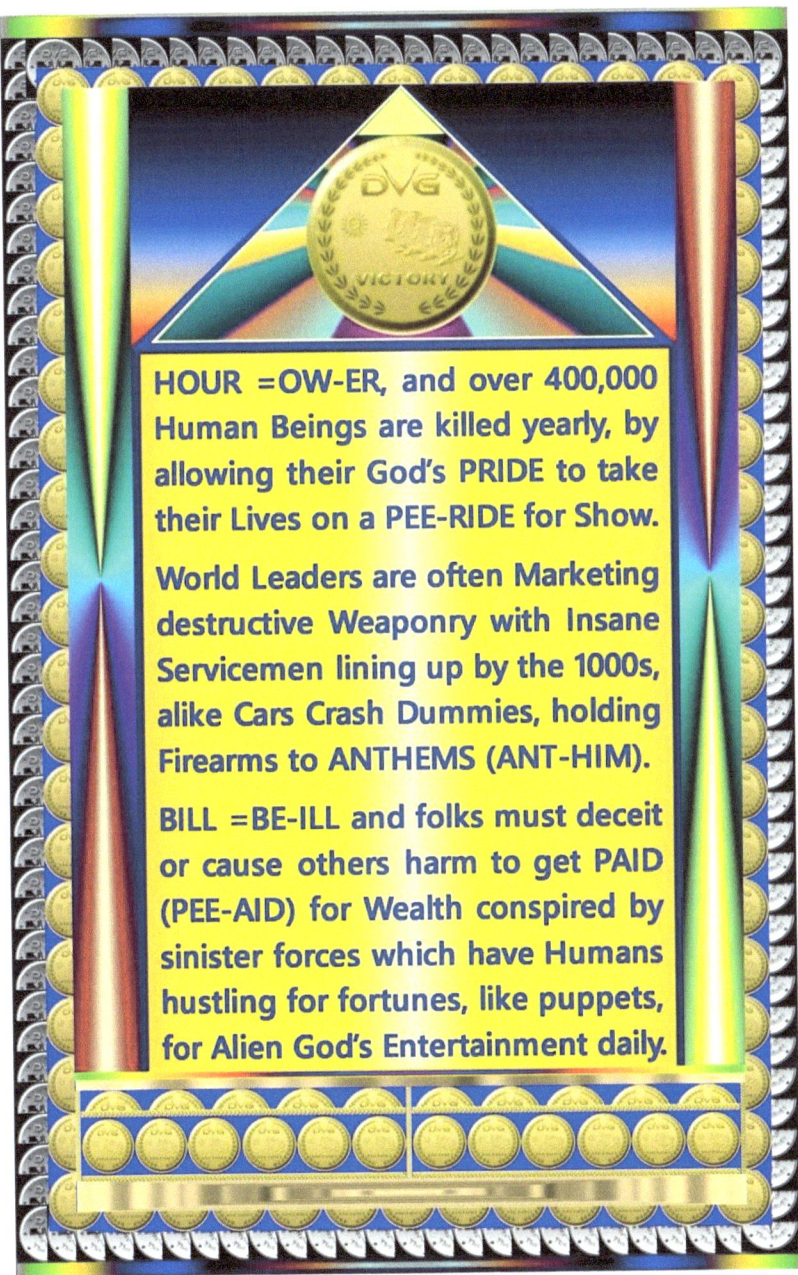

HOUR =OW-ER, and over 400,000 Human Beings are killed yearly, by allowing their God's PRIDE to take their Lives on a PEE-RIDE for Show.

World Leaders are often Marketing destructive Weaponry with Insane Servicemen lining up by the 1000s, alike Cars Crash Dummies, holding Firearms to ANTHEMS (ANT-HIM).

BILL =BE-ILL and folks must deceit or cause others harm to get PAID (PEE-AID) for Wealth conspired by sinister forces which have Humans hustling for fortunes, like puppets, for Alien God's Entertainment daily.

Humankind must do better at excelling our Youth. A Newborn Baby Brain is Incandescent, and should be taught more, energetically, before this activity starts to fade, at five years old, for Optimum Intelligence.

Today, Humankind come together, by the billions, to watch Athletes Injure and Demolition their Health in Sports daily. But we must realize that these are Dolt Acts and shouldn't be worthy of Human Admiration.

Forthcoming, I believe seeing folks achieving Health Persistence and the Quest of Humanity excelling to advanced Longevity, should be what's Praised daily.

Closing: I would like to remind Humanity that Alien God's prevent people from progressing by using dolt products like Gold and Oil as Fortune Bait every day.

Unfortunately, most Human's are in a rush to Pollute their own Air, Oceans, and sell Demolition Products, designed to hamper our Health, for this CON today.

Today, a World Leader has the highest Security daily, because they Dictate a CON Government and have to live in fear, of their closer peers, which is sad to see. We must take steps to eradicate all destructive actions caused from CON for profit, before Nuclear Weapons are exploded over everyone, any day, now.

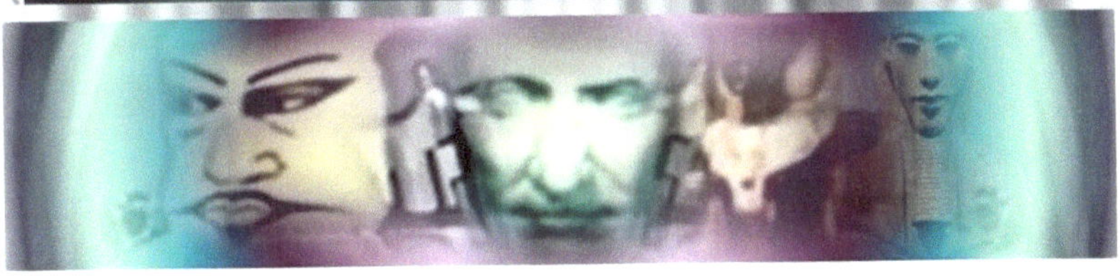

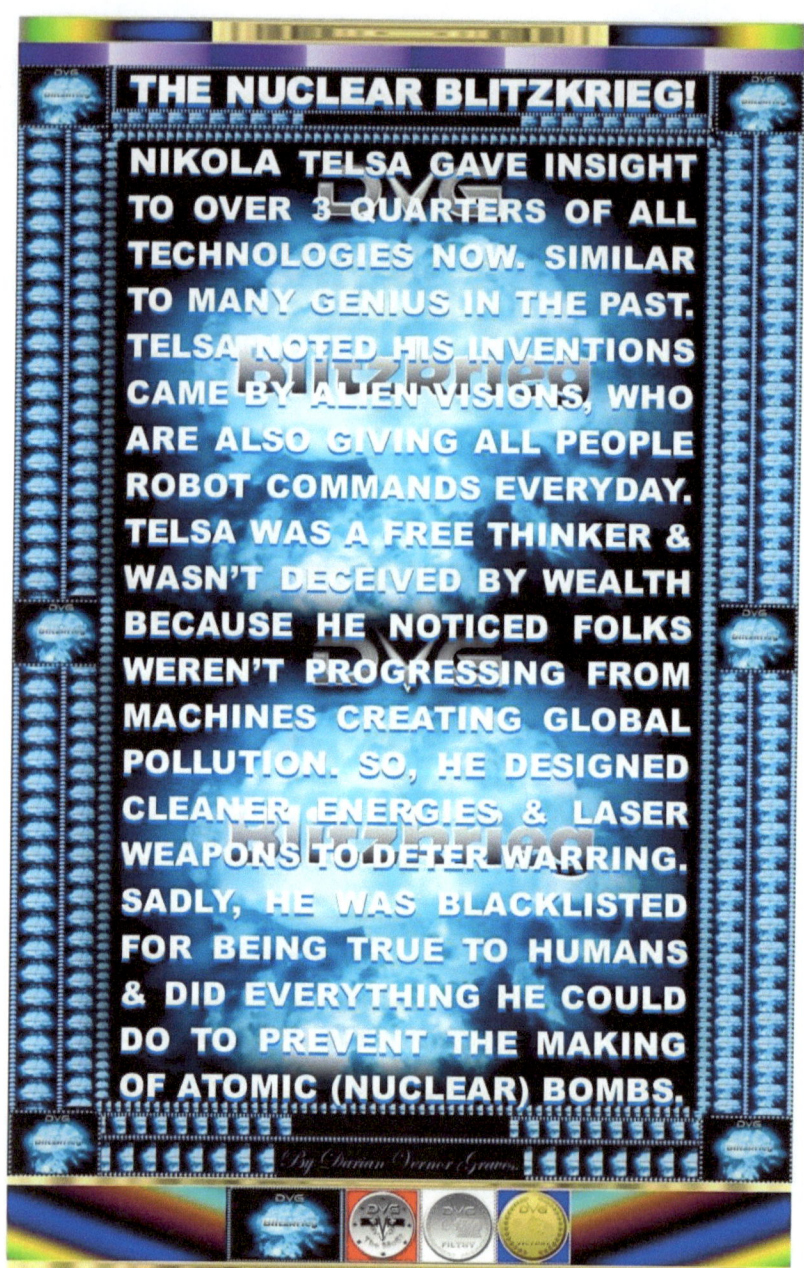

THE NUCLEAR BLITZKRIEG!

NIKOLA TELSA GAVE INSIGHT TO OVER 3 QUARTERS OF ALL TECHNOLOGIES NOW. SIMILAR TO MANY GENIUS IN THE PAST. TELSA NOTED HIS INVENTIONS CAME BY ALIEN VISIONS, WHO ARE ALSO GIVING ALL PEOPLE ROBOT COMMANDS EVERYDAY. TELSA WAS A FREE THINKER & WASN'T DECEIVED BY WEALTH BECAUSE HE NOTICED FOLKS WEREN'T PROGRESSING FROM MACHINES CREATING GLOBAL POLLUTION. SO, HE DESIGNED CLEANER ENERGIES & LASER WEAPONS TO DETER WARRING. SADLY, HE WAS BLACKLISTED FOR BEING TRUE TO HUMANS & DID EVERYTHING HE COULD DO TO PREVENT THE MAKING OF ATOMIC (NUCLEAR) BOMBS.

By Darian Vernor Graves.

THE NUCLEAR BLITZKRIEG!

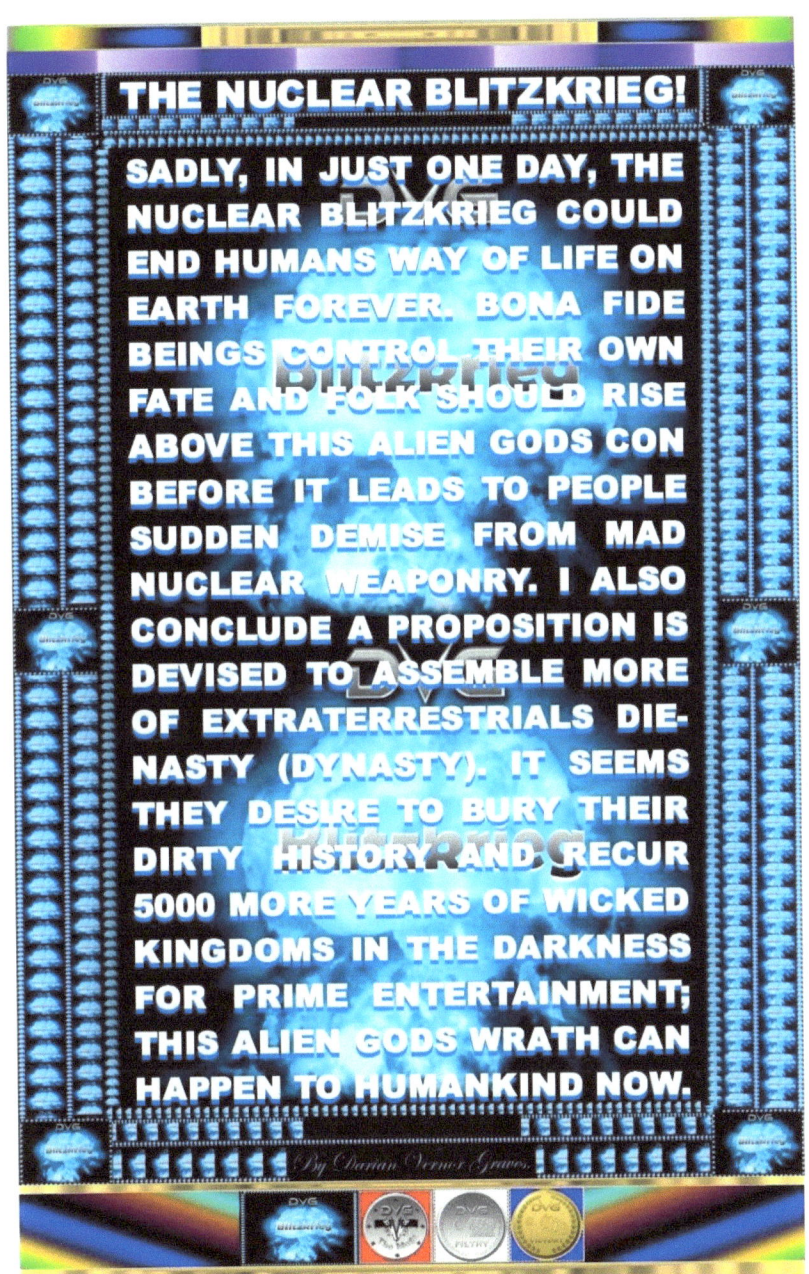

SADLY, IN JUST ONE DAY, THE NUCLEAR BLITZKRIEG COULD END HUMANS WAY OF LIFE ON EARTH FOREVER. BONA FIDE BEINGS CONTROL THEIR OWN FATE AND FOLK SHOULD RISE ABOVE THIS ALIEN GODS CON BEFORE IT LEADS TO PEOPLE SUDDEN DEMISE FROM MAD NUCLEAR WEAPONRY. I ALSO CONCLUDE A PROPOSITION IS DEVISED TO ASSEMBLE MORE OF EXTRATERRESTRIALS DIE-NASTY (DYNASTY). IT SEEMS THEY DESIRE TO BURY THEIR DIRTY HISTORY AND RECUR 5000 MORE YEARS OF WICKED KINGDOMS IN THE DARKNESS FOR PRIME ENTERTAINMENT; THIS ALIEN GODS WRATH CAN HAPPEN TO HUMANKIND NOW.

By Darian Vernor Graves.

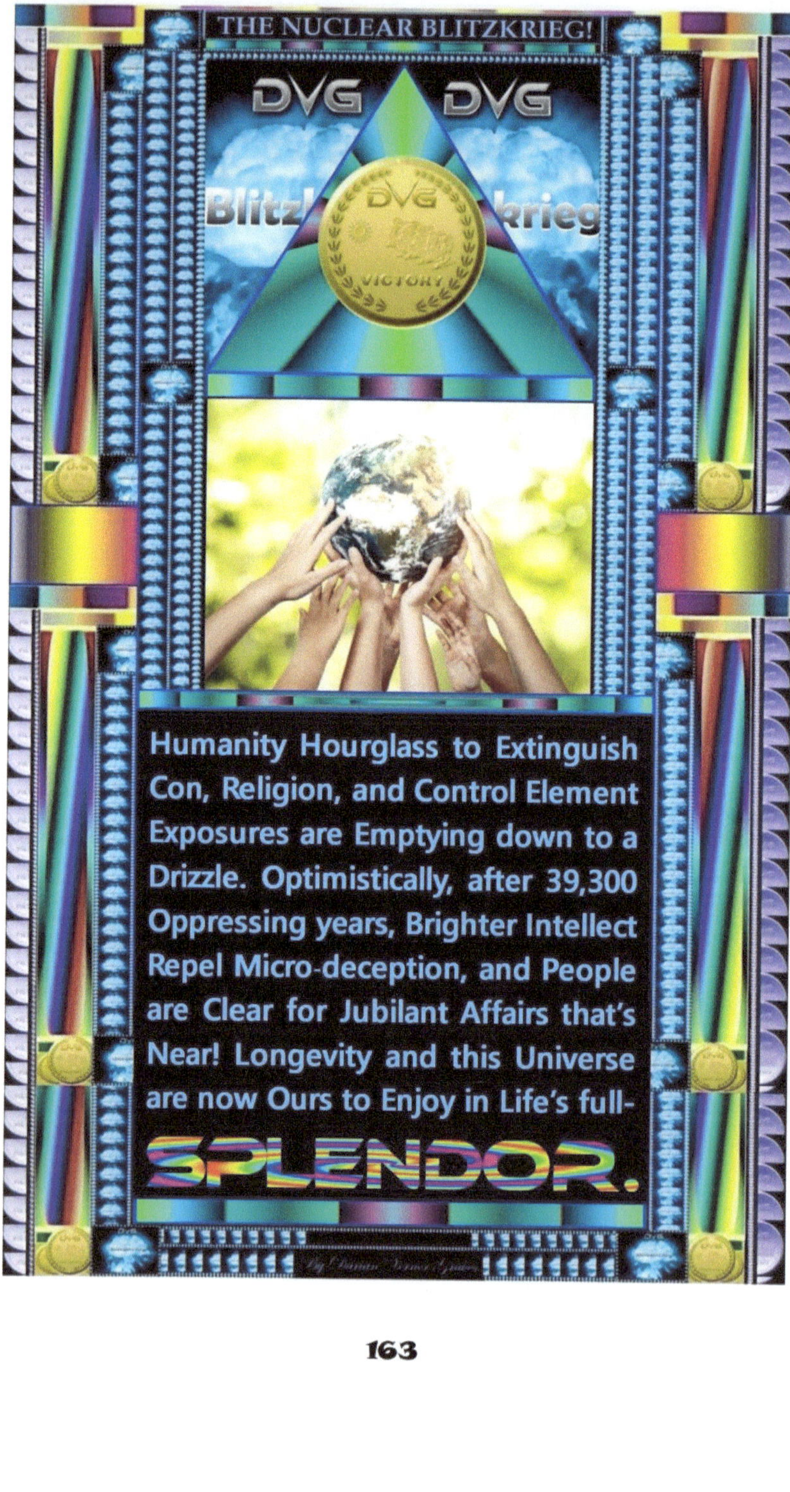
THE NUCLEAR BLITZKRIEG!
DVG
DVG
Blitz
krieg
DVG
VICTORY
Humanity Hourglass to Extinguish Con, Religion, and Control Element Exposures are Emptying down to a Drizzle. Optimistically, after 39,300 Oppressing years, Brighter Intellect Repel Micro-deception, and People are Clear for Jubilant Affairs that's Near! Longevity and this Universe are now Ours to Enjoy in Life's full-
SPLENDOR.

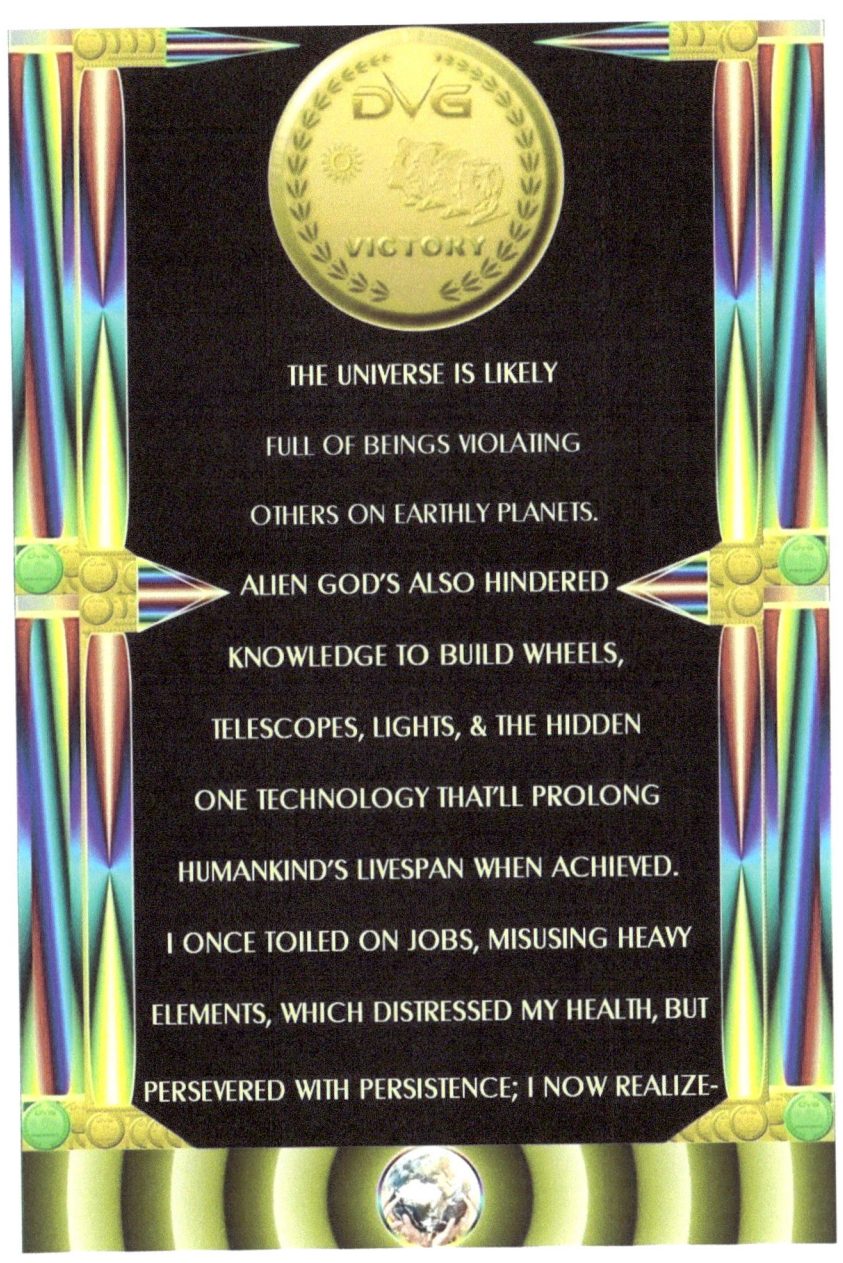

THE UNIVERSE IS LIKELY

FULL OF BEINGS VIOLATING

OTHERS ON EARTHLY PLANETS.

ALIEN GOD'S ALSO HINDERED

KNOWLEDGE TO BUILD WHEELS,

TELESCOPES, LIGHTS, & THE HIDDEN

ONE TECHNOLOGY THAT'LL PROLONG

HUMANKIND'S LIVESPAN WHEN ACHIEVED.

I ONCE TOILED ON JOBS, MISUSING HEAVY

ELEMENTS, WHICH DISTRESSED MY HEALTH, BUT

PERSEVERED WITH PERSISTENCE; I NOW REALIZE-

-WE
HAVE
ONLY ONE
OPTION IN LIFE
AND THAT'S TO LIVE:
HOW LONG AND HOW WE
LIVE ARE CHOSEN, WHICH CAN
END IN MORTALITY, OR THE LATTER
-Persistence.
FILTHY
VICTORY
DVG
PERSISTENCE

INDEX

SEE FOOTNOTES & ADDITIONAL RESOURCES
ON OUR WEBSITE: WWW.THEAFRICANTRUTH.COM

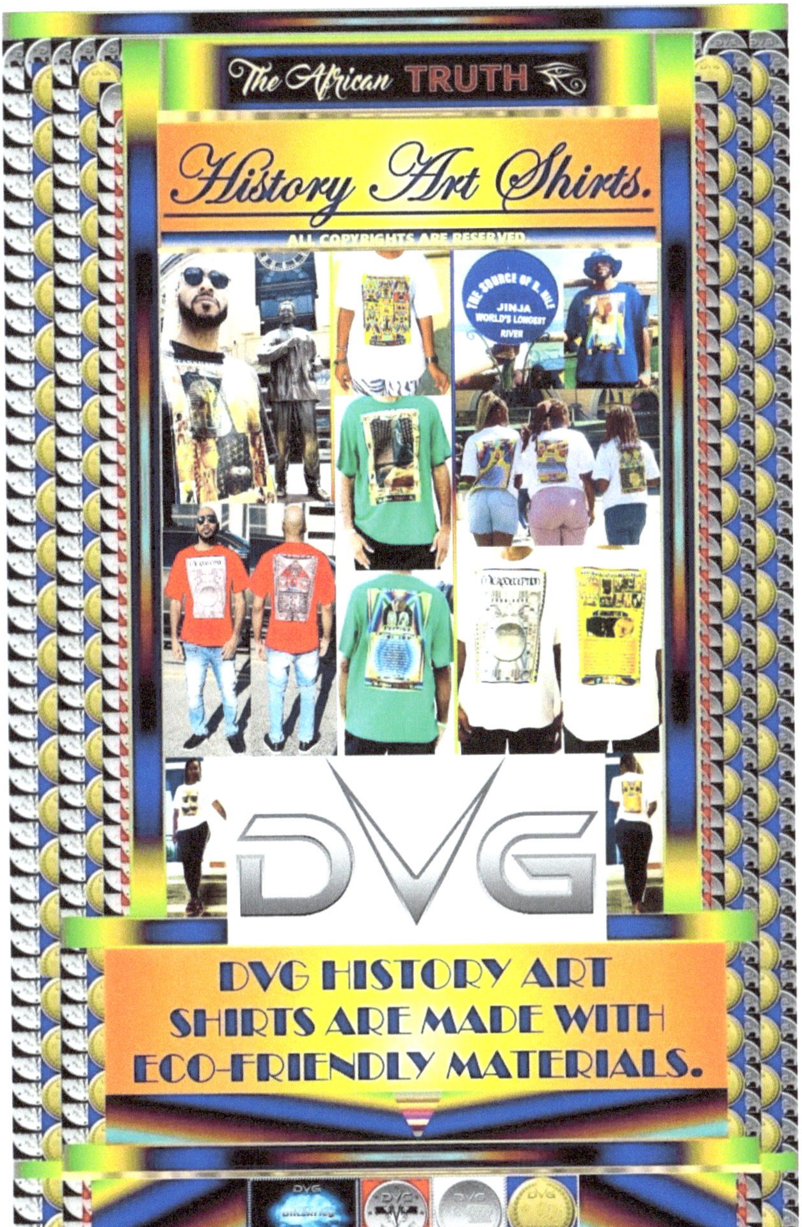
The African TRUTH
History Art Shirts.
ALL COPYRIGHTS ARE RESERVED.
THE SOURCE OF R. NILE
JINJA
WORLD'S LONGEST
RIVER
DVG
DVG HISTORY ART
SHIRTS ARE MADE WITH
ECO-FRIENDLY MATERIALS.

www.ingramcontent.com/pod-product-compliance
Lightning Source LLC
Chambersburg PA
CBHW042043290426
44109CB00001B/9
* 9 7 8 0 5 7 8 7 4 4 1 5 5 *